BETWEEN
TWO
WORLDS

· THE MEMOIRS OF STANLEY FROLICK ·

BETWEEN TWO WORLDS

• THE MEMOIRS OF STANLEY FROLICK •

Edited by
Lubomyr Y. Luciuk and Marco Carynnyk

The Multicultural History Society of Ontario
1990

This is a volume in the MHSO series Ethnocultural Voices

The Multicultural History Society of Ontario is a resource centre on the campus of the University of Toronto. It was created in 1976 by a group of academics, civil servants, librarians and archivists who saw a need for a special effort to preserve materials relevant to the province's immigrant and ethnic history. The Society receives support from the Ministry of Culture and Communications of the Province of Ontario, the Honourable Christine E. Hart, Minister.

Canadian Cataloguing in Publication Data

Frolick, Stanley, d. 1988
    Between two worlds

(Ethnocultural voices)
ISBN 0-919045-41-3

1. Frolick, Stanley, d. 1988.   2. Ukraine, Western - Politics and government.   3. Orhanizaﾃsiﾃa ukrainskykh natsionalistiv - Biography.   4. Ukrainian Canadians - Ukraine, Western - Biography.
5. Ukrainian Canadians - Manitoba - Biography.
I. Luciuk, Lubomyr Y., 1953-   . II. Carynnyk, Marco.
III. Multicultural History Society of Ontario.
IV. Title.   V. Series.

DK508.9.U37F76 1990   947'.718084'092   C90-093525-1

Design: Steve Eby

Published 1990

Printed and bound in Canada

CONTENTS

PREFACE

The experiences of immigrants and members of ethnic groups are raw material for historians, but they are also much more. Told in the voices of the individuals themselves, in memoirs, diaries, autobiographies and reminiscences, they have an immediacy that no third-person account can match. They kindle our imaginations and touch our hearts. For this reason the series Ethnocultural Voices while it contributes to scholarly study of ethnocultural history also increases public awareness and understanding of the diverse origins and experiences of Ontario's peoples.

The Multicultural History Society of Ontario has already published in the series *Heroes of Their Day: the Reminiscences of Bohdan Panchuk*, edited with an introduction by Lubomyr Luciuk. Now it presents the autobiography of Stanley Frolick, who participated in some of the same activities as Panchuk but whose background and point of view were quite different. Both Panchuk and Frolick exemplify in their careers Lord Tweedsmuir's statement, "You will all be better Canadians for being also good Ukrainians." The statement, made long before the word multiculturalism was coined, catches admirably the spirit of today's multicultural Canada, in which all of the different ethnic origins represented in the population are deemed worthy of celebration in a strong and developing nation.

The Multicultural History Society of Ontario is grateful to Lubomyr Luciuk and Marco Carynnyk for the care with which they have distilled from many hours of interviews the record of the background and early career of a remarkable Canadian.

JEAN BURNET

Multicultural History
Society of Ontario
1990

INTRODUCTION

Memoirs seldom say all. The remarkable story that Stanley Frolick set out to tell in this book – that of a boy from Alberta who grew up in Western Ukraine in the 1930s, took part in some of the most momentous events in Ukrainian and Ukrainian-Canadian history in the 1940s and then achieved a distinguished career in law and community service – is unfinished for three reasons.

Frolick began to chronicle his life in October 1981, when he completed the first of many hours of tape-recorded interviews. He participated in further sessions in 1983 and 1984, and then again in 1988. By then he was suffering from pulmonary fibrosis, and although he faced his ordeal stoically and strove to co-operate with us in the editing of his reminiscences, it was obvious that he would not be able to answer further questions or to work on the transcripts of earlier interviews. He died in Toronto on 4 June 1988.

The second reason for the gaps in Frolick's recollections is that from the mid-1930s until the early 1950s he was a member of the Organization of Ukrainian Nationalists.[1] Sworn to secrecy, he refused to say more than he absolutely had to when he was asked

---

1. The Organization of Ukrainian Nationalists, or OUN, was founded in 1929 as a revolutionary movement dedicated to the struggle for Ukrainian independence. In the autumn of 1942 the OUN gave rise to the Ukrainian Insurgent Army, or UPA, which mounted armed resistance to both the Nazis and the Soviets, and a year later to the Supreme Ukrainian Liberation Council, or UHVR. In the fall and winter of 1939-1940 the OUN split into two rival factions, known after their leaders, Stepan Bandera and Andrii Melnyk, as the *Banderivtsi*, or Banderites (OUN-B), and the *Melnykivtsi*, or Melnykites (OUN-M). For histories of the OUN see John A. Armstrong, *Ukrainian Nationalism* (New York: Columbia University Press, 1963); Alexander J. Motyl, *The Turn to the Right: The Ideological Origins and Development of Ukrainian Nationalism, 1919-1929* (Boulder: East European Monographs, 1980); and Peter J. Potichnyj and Yevhen Shtendera, eds., *Political Thought of the Ukrainian Underground, 1943-1951* (Edmonton: Canadian Institute of Ukrainian Studies, 1986).

questions about the OUN, even when they were based on archival materials unearthed in London, Ottawa, Toronto or Winnipeg and even though he would have done no harm by talking candidly about his work in the organization. Of course, he did not deny that he had been a member: that information, as he recounts in this book, had been leaked in the fall of 1946 and was discussed in Bohdan Panchuk's *Heroes of Their Day*.[2] Furthermore, Frolick's role in the founding of the League for the Liberation of Ukraine and the newspaper *Homin Ukrainy*, both of which are affiliated with the OUN, are matters of public record. One can admire the man's loyalty to his oath and yet regret that it deprived historians of insights into the workings of a movement that has struggled for Ukrainian independence for six decades.

The third reason why this book cannot claim to be a finished memoir is that in the interviews Frolick dealt largely with his life until the early 1950s, to the almost total exclusion of his later years in law and public affairs. Part of his story and part of the history of the Ukrainian diaspora are now forever lost.

In editing the transcripts, therefore, we consulted Frolick's personal papers and incorporated portions of his own articles, as well as passages from the autobiography that he intermittently worked on.[3] We have tried to retain Frolick's words and meaning and have included a number of photographs, most of them previously unpublished, that portray some of the people and places of his life.

---

2. *Heroes of Their Day: The Reminiscences of Bohdan Panchuk.* Edited and with an introduction by Lubomyr Y. Luciuk. Toronto: Multicultural History Society of Ontario and the Ontario Heritage Foundation, 1983.

3. The interviews listed below have been deposited with the Multicultural History Society of Ontario in Toronto, where they may be consulted by scholars who are interested in the events and people described in this book: Zoriana Sokolsky, June, August and September 1978 (UKR-8759-FRO); Lubomyr Luciuk, July 1981 (UKR-11337-FRO); Luciuk, October-November 1981, December 1983 and January 1984 (UKR-15500-FRO); and Lubomyr Luciuk and Marco Carynnyk, May 1988 (UKR-15501-FRO). Frolick also deposited with the MHSO three undated tapes detailing particular episodes in his life (UKR-15502-FRO). Additional tapes involving Frolick are on deposit with the Canadian Institute of Ukrainian Studies in Edmonton.

We are grateful to Dr. Oleh Romanyshyn and the Ucrainica Research Institute, Alexandra Chyczij, Edward and Anne Topornicki and the staff of the Multicultural History Society of Ontario for their help in the preparation of this manuscript. In particular we acknowledge the support of the late Professor Robert Harney who recognized the importance of capturing for posterity the experiences and perspectives of men like Stanley Frolick. And, finally, we thank the Frolick family, whose life we interrupted so often over the years to interview Stanley Frolick.

Frolick himself chose *Between Two Worlds* as the title of these reminiscences, in order, as he wrote, "to emphasize that what I am today is the result of having lived in two countries – Canada and Ukraine – which had different but equally significant influences on my growth, development and choice of a path in life. The title describes that hybrid creature – a Ukrainian Canadian who is not of the dominant Anglo-Celtic group and yet is also not wholly Ukrainian." Having worked for the independence of his ancestral land and for the betterment of the country he was born in, Stanley Frolick remained to the very end a patriot of both Ukraine and Canada. He may have been caught between two worlds, but his commitments remained undivided. For him this was the honourable way to live one's life.

LYL
MC
Toronto 1990

CHAPTER 1

ROOTS

In the early spring of 1910, tearful farewells were being said at the railway station in the town of Chernivtsi, capital of the Austro-Hungarian province of Bukovyna. A large group of Ukrainian peasants stood on the station platform – parents, brothers, sisters and assorted kinfolk, all from the village of Karliv – to see seven of their young men off on a journey across the continent and beyond the ocean into a remote corner of western Canada. The parting was much like the scene described by Vasyl Stefanyk in "The Stone Cross," except that on this occasion the leave-taking aroused even greater emotions because the emigrants were young lads between the ages of sixteen and twenty-two.[4] One of those seven young men was Yurii Froliak, my father. He was twenty-two years old.

The history of the Froliak family in Ukraine had begun with my great-great-grandfather, Danylo Fröhlich, a German colonist who had arrived in the village of Karliv shortly after the French Revolution. He was buried in that village, and I visited his grave, which is marked with a stone cross, but never thought of photographing his final resting place. He was a tall, well-built man known for the "European" clothes, and especially the bow-tie, that he always wore, in contrast to the local garb of white linen shirt and trousers. He lived for eighty-seven years. Being a German, he was a free man, and none of his direct descendants were serfs. Danylo left three sons: Mykola, who in turn had two sons and five daughters, Ivan, who had six sons and two daughters, and my great-grandfather Pavlo, who had six sons – Semen, Petro, Onufrii, Ivan, Yurii and my grandfather Mykhailo. Pavlo inherited the family house and holdings, which consisted of two farms with

---

4. Vasyl Stefanyk, *The Stone Cross* (Toronto: McClelland and Stewart, 1971).

1

thirty-six acres of land. He married a girl from the Lutsyk family in the neighbouring village of Rusiv (where Vasyl Stefanyk was born).

My grandfather recalled the festivities that marked the abolition of serfdom in 1848. There was much drinking and dancing in all the villages of Western Ukraine. For many years the peasants celebrated the anniversary, and even my father remembered observing people dancing and singing on that day beside the monument, a huge mound of earth topped by a cross that had been erected near the highway. When the Russian armies occupied Western Ukraine during the First World War, for some inexplicable reason they pulled down the cross and levelled the mound.

My grandfather also recalled that when he was a young boy there were crop failures for several years because of excessive rain. Famine stalked the land. The only work was on the construction of the first railway. The pay was two loaves of bread for a full day's work, and even then more workers volunteered than were required. The famine had ill effects on the fortunes of the Froliak clan. My great-grandfather traded ten acres to a landowner in the village of Ustia for thirty measures of potatoes so that he could seed his remaining land, and relatives in Rusiv, where conditions were not as bad as in Karliv, took my grandfather into their home.

The lean years were followed by years of good weather and excellent crops. In their joy the people began drinking to excess. Many peasants lost their land to money-lenders. A dedicated priest who had recently taken over the parish reversed this alarming trend. Father Andrii Voievidka was a member of *Vidrodzhennia*, or *"Renascence,"* an anti-smoking and anti-drinking society that was concerned not so much with health as with attacking the government monopoly on tobacco and alcohol. He ordered all the villagers over the age of eighteen to gather at the church, where he administered to them a sacred oath to abstain from alcohol. A great ceremony accompanied the oath. First a huge hole was dug. Then an oak whiskey cask was placed on a wagon drawn by my great-grandfather's four oxen. My grandfather Mykhailo and my great-uncle Petro drove the oxen from the church to the pit. Led by the priest, who was wearing his best vestments, the villagers followed the wagon, carrying crosses and church flags. When the procession arrived at the pit, the whiskey cask was thrown in and the villagers spat after it. Then the pit was filled and topped with a mound of earth on which an iron cross made by the local blacksmith was erected. Finally a picket fence was built around the mound and Lombardy poplars were planted in each corner.

Just before my father left Karliv in 1910, another mound was erected to honour the Ukrainian poet Taras Shevchenko. My father helped by transporting soil to the site in his wagon. The Russians levelled this mound as well during the First World War.

Another man who earned the villagers' respect was the teacher Makarevych. There was no school in the village, and Makarevych taught children in his own home, but because school attendance was not compulsory he had difficulty getting the children to attend. My grandfather used to tell me that Makarevych would drag children into his house to teach them to read and write. Whenever the boys and girls came face to face with him, they would jump over fences and run off to avoid being dragooned into school. My grandfather told this story with great sorrow: although his father and grandfather had been literate, he could barely sign his name. In 1909, after Makarevych died, the village built a magnificent brick church on the site of his house. Each villager contributed what he could in money or labour. The nearest railway station was three kilometres away in the village of Vydiniv, and my grandfather's contribution was to transport two carloads of bricks from the station to the church site. The labour he was donating was my father's.

At the turn of the century, the village had fifteen hundred inhabitants, who owned a thousand acres in the village itself and another five hundred acres in the village of Ustia on the other side of the Prut river. According to the electoral law, which allowed one representative for every five hundred inhabitants, the village elected three representatives. They in turn elected deputies to the provincial parliament in Lviv and the imperial parliament in Vienna. In 1902, the electoral law was changed to permit universal suffrage and the secret ballot, and the deputies to the provincial and imperial parliaments were elected directly. It was a source of great pride for the people of Karliv that the first peasant deputy to the parliament in Vienna from Western Ukraine was a man from their village named Ivan Sanduliak.

Karliv lay in the south-eastern corner of Western Ukraine, in a region known as Pokuttia, which embraced the counties of Kolomyia, Sniatyn and Horodenka. Under Soviet rule, the village was renamed Prutivka because it lies on the Prut river. Pokuttia had a well-developed agriculture and by the time of my father's departure for Canada had attained a high degree of political and national consciousness. Socialism was the spirit of the times, and one of its manifestations was the Ukrainian Radical Party, which was well-entrenched in Pokuttia. In part this was because such leading figures in the socialist movement as Mykhailo Pavlyk and Kyrylo Tryliovsky came from the region. By the turn of the century, after the right wing had split away to form the Ukrainian National Democratic Party and the left had formed the Ukrainian Social Democratic Party, the Ukrainian Radical Party had lost its monopoly but was still pre-eminent in Pokuttia.

My great-grandfather's wife was gored to death by a bull. Within a year his brother Ivan found him a second wife in the neighbouring village of Zaluche. My great-grandfather went by ox-wagon to marry the bride he had never seen. It is said that a different girl appeared at the altar. The substitution was discovered only after the wedding. My great-grandfather was so mortified by the thought that he had been made a fool that he committed suicide within two years. My grandfather Mykhailo was taken in by his mother's family, the Lutsyks, in the village of Rusiv. Vasyl Lutsyk became the guardian of Pavlo's underage children, took over his land and divided it equally between the four sons. As soon as Mykhailo reached the age of eighteen his guardian told him that a woman was required in the household and ordered him to get married. Mykhailo married a seventeen-year-old girl from a good family whose two brothers were serving as non-commissioned officers in the Austro-Hungarian army. Three sons were born of that marriage: Vasyl, my father Yurii, or Yurko, and Ivan, who died in infancy of measles. Grandmother was a hard-working and religious woman who lavished much love on her children. The family prospered. When he had finished the village school, Vasyl was enrolled in a *gymnasium* in Kolomyia.

That was when the trouble started. With her eldest son away, grandmother was overcome by grief and loneliness. She cried and worried about Vasyl's welfare and begged her husband to bring him back. Grandfather finally relented, harnessed a team of horses to the wagon and went to Kolomyia to bring Vasyl home. But he returned without Vasyl, having changed his mind and believing that he was doing best by giving Vasyl a good education. He promised my father that he, too, would go to the *gymnasium* in Kolomyia. That was not to be, however, because grandmother succumbed to her grief and became mentally ill. Grandfather called in doctors, but the state of medicine in the rural regions of Western Ukraine at that time was such that they could do little. Grandfather then turned to the village healer. The unfortunate woman was tied to a pear tree, and a young boy was sent to the top of the tree with a bucket of cold water and told to pour it on her head. Her condition deteriorated. Although she had lucid moments, she was often violent and failed to recognize anyone except Yurko. She was taken to hospitals in Sniatyn and Chernivtsi, but they would not admit her. To keep her from harming herself, holes were drilled through the sideboards of the bed, ropes were inserted and her arms and legs were tied down. She pulled at the ropes so frantically that she rubbed her ankles and wrists raw. The poor woman suffered. So did her family. The only person who could feed her was my father. Father and son wept bitterly. One had lost a wife, the other a mother. Things went from bad to worse. After two years my grandfather managed to have his wife admitted to the mental hospital in Lviv. She died there shortly thereafter.

My grandfather fell into a deep apathy. His farm was going to ruin. He kept selling pieces of land and even some farm buildings. My father cried and tried to remember the loving mother who was no more. My grandfather resisted all pleas to get back on his feet and to remarry. There was only one cow left, and my father, who was nine years old, had to clean, feed and milk it. To save the family from utter ruin, my grandfather's brothers and cousins finally forced him to remarry. They found an eighteen-year-old girl from the Semeniuk family. Things took an immediate turn for the better. The new wife was industrious and thrifty. Soon three additional children were born, and my father, having finished the grade school in the village, could not be spared to go to the *gymnasium* in Kolomyia. He not only had to look after his half-sisters while his father and stepmother were working in the fields, but had to tend the farm animals, the garden and the orchard. My father wistfully wrote in his diary that he lost the name Yurko and was known as the *chort*, or devil. His stepmother became violently antagonistic towards him. Although she was only eight years older than my father, she frequently beat him. He never raised his hand in self-defence. The church taught that one must not resist a parent, even a wicked stepmother.

Young Yurko had long, curly hair. One day another boy made fun of his hair and called him a sheep. The boys scuffled and then went home. From the barn where he was doing his chores Yurko noticed the other boy's father coming over to complain. When he went into the house, his stepmother accused him of eating good food and being a good-for-nothing who beat up other children. Picking up the mangle with which she had been washing clothes, she knocked him to the floor. Then she jumped on the boy and, although she was pregnant at the time, pummeled him with such vigour that her water sack broke and showered him with its contents. To get away, Yurko rolled under the bed. She seized a spindle and attempted to stab him. But he grabbed hold of it and would not let go. She shook with fury. "Wait till your father gets home!" she threatened. "He'll break every bone in your body!" Back in the barn, Yurko observed his father coming home. He approached the house quietly to listen to what was being said inside. "Kill him!" his stepmother was raving. "Kill him! He's no good!" His father did not answer.

When Yurko came into the house, his father asked him why his shirt was torn.

"Mother hit me across the back with the mangle and then tried to stab me with the spindle," he replied.

His father turned to his wife. "You will kill a good worker." Then he addressed the boy. "Go and groom the horses." As the boy was going out, he said to his wife, "Why do you pick on him? You often pick on him for no reason at all."

By this time Yurko's brother Vasyl had enrolled in the faculty of law at Lviv University. He studied at home and went to the university at the end of every semester to take his exams. He often found Yurko crying. "He knew that I was the victim of our stepmother's inexplicable hatred," my father told me. "But he cautioned me not to lay a hand on her as otherwise father would renounce me and ask me to leave home. He comforted me, advised me to be patient until he had finished his law course, established himself as a lawyer and could take me to live with him. 'Then we'll eat white buttered bread and drink coffee with cream and sugar,' he would say. Indeed I found comfort in those words and resolved to bear my tribulations in silence. I guess my stepmother resented the fact that I had inherited from my mother four acres of good land that she coveted for herself and her children."

In 1907, when he was nineteen, my father became a teamster and hired himself and his wagon and horses to anyone who required such service. Now he was away from his stepmother much of the time, and although he turned over his wages to his father he was sometimes able to keep a few crowns for himself. He was a good worker, and many a mother in the village had an eye on him as a husband for her daughter. One such girl was comely seventeen-year-old Anna, but all the attempts at matchmaking were frustrated by Yurko's resolve not to get married. He was dreaming of going to Canada and earning enough money to come back, buy additional land, build a house and start his own farm. Undeterred, Anna's mother went to talk with Yurko's parents. She offered to arrange the wedding and to pay for everything. Yurko's stepmother flew into a rage, told her to get out of the house and announced that she would not permit Yurko either to get married or to emigrate to Canada. He was required at home as a provider.

The stepmother was also hostile to Vasyl, but, because of the esteem in which higher education was held, he endured much less abuse from her than Yurko. Perhaps the fact that he was only four years younger than his stepmother also restrained her. Nevertheless, he found it difficult to find sufficient funds for his studies, and had it not been for Yurko, who occasionally slipped him two or three crowns from the money he earned as a teamster, things would have been much worse. After Vasyl completed the *gymnasium* he was called up for military service and served as a second lieutenant with the Tyrolean sharpshooters. Yurko felt very proud when his brother came home on leave, splendidly attired in his officer's uniform. He would take his brother's sword out of the scabbard, flash it and make thrusts and parries at imaginary enemies.

In March 1908 Yurko came home from a dance late one evening and before retiring went into the stable to throw down hay for the horses and oxen. A horse kicked him in the left leg just above the knee, breaking the bone. The village healer placed leeches on the ugly bruise. When they had gorged themselves with blood and fallen off, he crushed charcoal into a powder and applied it to the wounds left by the leeches. After three weeks, Yurko was able to walk again, although the bones had not been set properly and the left leg was now shorter than the right. This may have been a blessing in disguise: when he was called up for military service the following year, he was pronounced unfit for duty.

When the prospect of military service was no longer hanging over his head, Yurko asked his father for money to go to Canada. His father readily consented, went to the bank to make arrangements and was told that his wife's signature would be required on the promissory note. She adamantly refused to sign. Even my grandfather's attempt to play on her hostile feelings towards her stepson was unsuccessful. "You have nothing to lose by letting him go to Canada," he said to her. "At the very worst he will die there and leave his land." "No," she replied, "he's young, healthy and cunning. He'll survive, and without him who is going to help me bring up our children?"

Yurko was not to be denied his dream. He came to terms with two neighbours who had marriageable daughters. The neighbours would guarantee the loan for his trip, and when he returned to the village he would marry one of the daughters. So it was done. Yurko's father borrowed five hundred crowns from the bank, and the two neighbours co-signed the promissory note. For luck, Yurko's father added another ten crowns from his own pocket. Yurko went off to Chernivtsi to buy his ticket to Canada. He paid the Globe agency three hundred crowns for a ticket to Winnipeg. For seven crowns he bought himself a suit of clothes and a shirt. When he came home in the evening, his stepmother was asleep. His father sat up with him to give him his last admonishment.

"You are about to leave for a far-off land on the other side of the ocean," he said. "If you become ill or incapacitated, let me know and I will somehow bring you back. If you find a job, stick with it. Don't be a rolling stone that gathers no moss. Everyone respects a man who keeps his word and carries out his end of the bargain. Don't try to be the first, and also try not to be the last. Don't spend your money foolishly. Try to save as much money as you can for yourself. If you can send some money to me, that will be good. I'll need money because it is my intention to send all the children to school to get a higher education."

The next day Yurko went to say good-bye to his relatives and friends. He learned that his friends had arranged a mass to be celebrated for his safe journey. "You don't need to go," my grandfather said. "You can pray at home and use your time to bring a few wagonloads of earth that we'll need to repair the farm buildings." That was how my father spent his last day at home.

In the evening, his friends gathered, and one of them cut off his long hair. The party lasted into the small hours of the morning. Before he knew it, he was being shaken awake and told to have breakfast and get ready to go to the station. A crowd of people had gathered in the farmyard. A wagon was hitched, and sheaves of hay were placed inside and covered with linen to serve as seats. It was difficult to get out of the yard because the people would not let the wagon through.

This was the third departure for Canada from Karliv. The first was in 1904. My grandfather was to have left at that time, but his new wife would not hear of it. Three families departed on that occasion. In 1908 six people emigrated. This time seven young men were leaving.

When the train for Chernivtsi arrived in Zaluche at eight o'clock, a great cry went up from the crowd. Some people clung to the travellers to prevent them from leaving. The conductor blew his whistle again and again. Finally the train moved off. At the station in Chernivtsi five hundred people were waiting to start their journey to the unknown land.

As he was getting out of the wagon at the station in Zaluche Yurko had an embarrassing accident. The seat of his trousers split. "Don't worry," his father reassured him. "On the way from Chernivtsi the train will stop in Zaluche again, and I will bring your brother's trousers for you to put on."

When the train stopped in Zaluche, Yurko's stepmother passed him a pair of trousers through the window. Her final words were extraordinary. "Forgive me for everything and please don't forget us," she said.

Amid much crying and shouts of best wishes and farewell, the train rolled on to Kolomyia and then to Antwerp. My father described the voyage in his autobiography:

Upon reaching Antwerp, we were put into immigration sheds and kept there for four days and nights, and on 14 April 1910 we were taken under escort aboard a freighter that carried about three thousand passengers. The hold of the ship was not partitioned. Men were separated from women by canvas curtains hanging from the beams, and bunks were placed side by side, two high. This area in turn was separated from the eating area by another canvas curtain. There were three sittings at every meal, taken at long wooden trestle tables. The North Atlantic is rough at this time of year, and 1910 was no exception. People were tossed about in the hold of the ship. Many were seasick, and few had any appetite. All during the storm the immigrants were confined to the hold of the ship, and only on the eighth day, when the sea had calmed, were they allowed onto the deck. Conditions were so bad that one night water came into the hold and the passengers' trunks and suitcases were floating about.

I had forty dollars with me. On the thirteenth day of of our sea journey, someone stole my money. It was well known that on arrival in Halifax every passenger had to declare at least twenty-five dollars in his possession. Otherwise he was not permitted to land and was returned to Europe at the steamship company's expense. You can imagine my despair. For a while I considered jumping overboard and ending my life in the cold waters of the Atlantic. But help came from an unexpected source. I had mentioned the theft to a sailor. He reported it to the captain, who came into the hold and announced in three languages that money had been stolen from me. There were ways to identify the money, and if the thief failed to return it a search would be conducted the following morning and he would be arrested and handed over to the authorities in Halifax, where a jail sentence would await him. Much to my delight, when I awoke in the morning I found the money lying beside me on the bed.

After eighteen days and nights we docked in Halifax at ten o'clock in the morning on 2 May 1910. Before being processed by the immigration officials we had to show that we possessed at least twenty-five dollars. Out of the generosity of some unknown person or agency we were given sandwiches, apples, oranges and even tobacco in little cloth bags, and all this free of charge! Needless to say, all the passengers were greatly impressed with this welcome to the new land which indicated its generosity and wealth. Amidst much merriment the food was washed down with the home-made plum brandy that many of the passengers had in their luggage. Soon after, we climbed aboard the immigration cars on the train, which consisted of wooden benches and platforms suspended from the ceiling with chains on which baggage was placed and on which people slept at night, two to a platform. Three days later, towards evening, we arrived in Winnipeg and were greeted by a considerable number of Ukrainians.

I spent a week in Winnipeg. I met a friend from home, but was not impressed with him because he was poorly dressed in overalls, drank a lot and spent most of his time in pool halls. It was good to rest after the strenuous sea journey. A bed at that time cost ten cents a night. Breakfast, lunch and dinner also cost ten cents each. A large glass of beer was five cents and a shot of whiskey fifteen cents. As in Western movies, the bartender would place a shot glass and a bottle before the customer, who would pour his own drink. We made sure that the glass was filled to the brim.

I spent my time wandering through the city, window-shopping and even entering a few shops and looking into the possibility of finding a job in the city. One thing that particularly caught my fancy was a beautiful harness for horses which I decided I would buy to take home with me after I had earned enough money.

As far as employment was concerned, construction work was available at twenty cents an hour, but hod carriers could make twenty-five cents an hour by carrying bricks on their backs. The four of us from our village decided against taking a job and settling in Winnipeg, as we were sure that those who had preceded us to the Crow's Nest Pass in Alberta knew the situation much better than we did and that if they had passed up the chance to stay in Winnipeg the jobs must be better there.

Another factor in our decision to move west was that I had a cousin, Mykhailo Ostafiichuk, and my friend, Yurko Semotiuk, had a brother in those parts. We therefore paid a dollar each for a ticket to Medicine Hat in Alberta and from there transferred to the branch line running through McLeod, the Kootenays and on to Vancouver. From Medicine Hat we paid three cents a mile for the fare, but the carriages were much finer than the ones in which we had travelled from Halifax to Winnipeg. The seats were soft and upholstered in velvet, a luxury we could not have imagined.

The train approached the foothills of the Rockies, and we finally found ourselves in the heart of the mountains, encircled by towering snow-covered peaks. We disembarked at the station in Frank. Surrounded by wild forests and still wilder mountains, we looked at one another in dismay. "My God, how did we get here?"

The scene that confronted the Ukrainian boys was much as it is today. White limestone cliffs surround the hamlet of Frank, and beyond the station stretches an eerie, boulder-strewn landscape. The mass of rock, estimated to be a hundred million tons in all, fell from the steep east face of Turtle Mountain in April 1903, burying sixty-six people in the hamlet under a fifty-foot blanket of limestone boulders covering more than a square mile.[5]

Beyond the disaster area, dark, impenetrable forests stretch out in all directions, and craggy mountains reach for the sky. The contrast between the cultivated plains of Western Ukraine and these untamed forests and foreboding mountains was too great for the young immigrants to comprehend. They stood at the station overwhelmed by a feeling of having been abandoned and betrayed. Fear and homesickness clutched at their hearts. They broke down and cried. Their tears, soon to be followed by sweat and blood, watered the soil of their new land.

The shock of arrival in Frank was eased by Petro Trofan and Dmytro Sanduliak, both of whom were from Karliv and had settled in the Crow's Nest Pass. They arrived at the station shortly after the train had departed. They tried to reassure the new arrivals, distracting them with stories of life in the new country and questions about mutual friends at home.

"Wipe away your tears," they said. "Things aren't all that bad, and you'll get used to these new surroundings, but first let us treat you to some food and drink."

---

5. Y. Frolick, "The Horrible Tragedy in Hillcrest," *Ukrainian Life* vol. XXIV, no. 27, July 1, 1964, p. 5.

The group set out for the hotel. Later they went to Hillcrest, which was to be their new home, some four miles away. The road was rough and strewn with stones and boulders. Stumbling, falling, scraping and bruising their elbows and knees, the men finally reached their destination. At the house of one of the settlers they were met by people from Karliv: Semen Sanduliak, Petro Kostyniuk, Vasyl Semotiuk and Mykhailo Ostafiichuk. All of them worked on the same shift, from seven in the morning to three in the afternoon. Then two other shifts went down into the bowels of the mountains to dig for coal.

Yurko spent the night talking with his cousin Ostafiichuk. He had already resolved that he would return to Winnipeg, but his cousin argued against it. He pointed out that the pay in the coal mines was higher and that city life contained many pitfalls for a young and unsophisticated person. Besides, it would be better to stick together in Hillcrest where they could stand by each other and save money more easily than in the city. Yurko reluctantly agreed. He regretted that decision for many years. If he had gone to Winnipeg, he thought, he would have found a better job and would have learned more English than he did in Hillcrest, where he associated only with fellow Ukrainians.

The first few weeks in Hillcrest did not augur well for the future. In mid-May 1910 a general strike was called in the coal mines, and there was no immediate prospect of getting a job. But then a contractor set about building a branch line to Frank in order to smelt lime. Yurko was hired for his first job in Canada: loading limestone onto carts for twenty-five cents an hour.

At seven o'clock the next morning Yurko reported to the job site and began shovelling limestone. Distracted by the scenery and the work going on around him, he worked slowly and deliberately. He had noticed that the boss was watching him, but thought that he was admiring his work. During the lunch break, the boss called him over and handed him two dollars and fifty cents. This was Yurko's pay, and he had been fired.

Yurko was shocked and humiliated. He had always considered himself to be a good worker. Now he was worried about finding another job and surviving. Frightened and despondent, he went into the tall grass, lay down and cried. He did not want to go back to his cousin and friends in Hillcrest. But by evening he had gathered enough courage to face them. His cousin did not recriminate him and only suggested that he go to Fernie, in British Columbia, to look for a job and offered to accompany him.

When they arrived in Fernie, they found the buildings draped in bunting: King Edward VII had died. "On 21 May," my father wrote in his diary, "I was sent to Cranbrooke to apply for a job on a railway gang. The boss, a redheaded Scotsman, looked me over, felt the muscles on my arms and legs as if I were a horse at a market or a slave on a block, gave me a long, heavy crowbar and told me to remove old rails and to replace them with new ones."

The pay was twenty-seven cents an hour for a ten-hour work-day. The workers were housed in boxcars on a siding and received three meals a day for a price of sixty-five cents. This still left two dollars and five cents for a day's work. Yurko was pleased and worked willingly. Having been humiliated once, he was determined not to be fired again. The lesson was brought home even more forcibly when slack workers were fired immediately. If they dared to argue, the red-headed boss would send them on their way with a kick to the backside. Jobs were scarce, and with the miners out on strike and looking for employment, it was necessary to put up with a lot merely to hang on to one's job.

My father kept meticulous accounts all his life. He had complete records of all his earnings from his first day in Canada to his last. When he went on a trip, he wrote down when he left, how much his ticket cost and what he spent. He kept track of all the letters he wrote, the amounts he enclosed and the replies he received. His accounts show that he was careful with the money he earned and did not spend it on anything except food. By July he had repaid his father the $110 that his transportation to Canada had cost, and on 20 September he sent his father an additional $150 to help the family. He was rewarded with a letter from his stepmother who praised his generosity and said that not one person from the village had sent so much money in so short a time.

Between 1910 and 1926 my father sent his family $1,136. That was a lot of money for a family in a village in Western Ukraine. It was in great measure because of this financial assistance that Yurko's father was able to educate his children, all of whom completed *gymnasium* and in most cases university as well. The financial assistance continued until my father's death. Even his marriage in 1919 and the birth of two sons in 1920 and 1923 did not stop the flow of money to the old country.

In the fall of 1910, after four and a half months' work on the railway, Yurko received a letter from a friend in Fernie. The government was building a highway and paying thirty cents an hour. Yurko quit his job, bade his fellow workers farewell and with four others left Cranbrooke. The cook made sure that they were well supplied with food for their journey. To save money, they travelled by freight train. Sitting in an empty boxcar, they ate their sandwiches, joked and told stories. When the train stopped to take on water and coal, they would jump out for a drink of water. When fresh water was not available, they drank from the ditches along the tracks. By the time the train reached Fernie, the five men were running temperatures and barely made it to the house of a friend in the town.

Yurko willed himself to go to a store to buy a suit, two shirts, shoes, underwear, socks and a cap. He hoped that he would have a better chance of getting a job if he looked like a "Canadian." But his condition worsened, and he was taken to the private hospital in Fernie. The doctor who examined him told him that he had typhus. Having spent twenty dollars for clothing, my father had only forty dollars of his savings left. And the doctor was requiring twenty-five dollars a week to treat him. When the money ran out, the doctor asked whether Yurko had any relatives in Canada. Yurko replied that he had two cousins in Hillcrest. "In that case," the doctor said, "you will have to go to Hillcrest, where they can look after you."

His friends took him by wagon to the station and placed him on the train to Hillcrest. When he arrived there, no one was at the station. Unable to walk and not knowing where to go, Yurko lay on the station platform and cried.

A man who knew Yurko's cousin Ostafiichuk came by after a while. "As a matter of fact," he said, "I work with him smelting lime, and I'll help you to his place."

"The good man brought me to my cousins's room and put me to bed, and shortly thereafter my cousin came in," my father wrote.

On learning that I was sick with typhus, he went to the livery stable, hired a horse and wagon, spread straw in the wagon, came back and together with his friend put me on the bed of straw and covered me with blankets as I was shaking with fever. The doctor at the hospital in Frank refused to admit me if I could not pay twenty-five dollars a week. I had no money. Nor did my cousin, and all our pleas and promises to pay later were to no avail. Back we went to my cousin's shack.

The shack was owned by a Swedish foreman who had the job of setting dynamite charges in the limestone quarry. There were two beds occupied by four persons in the shack. The Swede looked me over, brought in a small cot and told me to lie down. Then he telephoned the RCMP in Frank to report that he had a man sick with typhus on his hands. Two mounted constables came by to investigate. They asked me where I had worked and when I had come to Canada and assured me that the government would look after me. No further action was taken, and I never heard from the mounted police or any other government agency again.

The next day the Swede told me that I would have to move because he and the others would be in trouble if I died and a corpse were found in the shack. Despite my fever and hallucinations, I discussed the matter with my cousin. In exchange for one acre of land from my inheritance he agreed to take me to a hospital and to assume responsibility for the cost. I was then taken to Dr. Wilson's hospital in Belleview.

Dr. Wilson had a hospital in one part of his house and lived in the other. He had no nurse. He agreed to take me in and look after me for fifteen dollars a week on the condition that my cousin would either stand duty at my bedside every night or would arrange for someone else to do so. Dr. Wilson would check on me periodically during the day, give me injections and pills and feed me.

About a week later I went into a coma. I have no way of knowing how long I remained in that state. But I vividly recall regaining consciousness and seeing four of my friends from my village, the doctor and a clergyman at my bedside. My friends told me that Dr. Wilson had sent an urgent message to them that I was dying and that they ought to come with a clergyman to pay their last respects. But I cheated death and came back to life. I was confined in Dr. Wilson's hospital for a total of seven weeks for which my cousin paid one hundred dollars. Dr. Wilson then brought me back to the shack. To help me convalesce he bought fishing rods for us, and we would sit on the riverbank fishing for trout, which were plentiful in the clear mountain water. On such occasions, Dr. Wilson would tell anyone willing to listen that he was a father to me because he had snatched me from the jaws of death and given me a new life.

By November 1910 I was well enough to go back to work. On 23 November I got a job filling barrels with lime that paid two dollars and fifty cents a day, but the dust from the lime was impossible to get used to and caused me great trouble. The strike in the coal mines lasted for six months. The strikers won an increase of five cents an hour, and on 1 December all of them went back to work. Those who were on piece-work were able to earn between one hundred and five hundred dollars a month. Those who were not on piece-work received three dollars a day for an eight-hour day.

On 1 January 1911, I got a job in the Hillcrest coal mine. My task was to carry props to the miners at the coal face to be used for shoring up the roof. I was paid two dollars and seventy-five cents a shift.

Near the mine there was a small frame cottage. The stable boss had lived there, but now it was empty. I asked the mine manager for permission to live in it. Permission was granted for annual payment of four dollars a month for the school tax and one dollar a month for electricity. The timekeeper prepared a lease for my signature, and I moved in with four friends. The cost of maintaining the house was minimal, as coal and wood for heating and cooking were free. Many meat items, such as liver, heart, pigs' feet and pigs' heads for making headcheese, were also free, and our food came to only seven or eight dollars a month. We took turns cooking and performing other household chores. We built a brick oven outside in which we baked bread.

That little house was possibly the first housing co-operative in Canada. Four-fifths of the Ukrainians in Hillcrest were bachelors, and my father, who was then the financial secretary of the Ukrainian Social Democratic Party (USDP) branch[6] in the town, proposed at a meeting that the single members organize a co-op and reduce their household chores. He was elected to be chairman and manager of the project. A Chinese cook was hired. He soon learned to prepare such Ukrainian dishes as *borshch*, *varenyky* and *holubtsi*. A photograph of the residents of the co-op with their cook taken in May 1918 bears a note by my father on the reverse:

The cook cooked and baked all sorts of food. The boys ate as much as they wanted. In the stores we were given monthly credit. The costs of the cook and the victuals were borne equally by all. All bills and receipts were kept in an accessible place for inspection by anyone who wanted to see them. We called this a co-operative. We

6. For histories of the Ukrainian-Canadian left see Peter Krawchuk, *The Ukrainian Socialist Movement in Canada (1907-1918)* (Toronto: Progress Books, 1979), and John Kolasky, *The Shattered Illusion: The History of Ukrainian Pro-Communist Organizations in Canada* (Toronto: PMA Books, 1979).

were known throughout the Crow's Nest Pass. We served as examples to other miners. We took turns keeping order. Drinking and gambling were prohibited. There was unity and mutual respect amongst us. I was made boss of the whole enterprise.

The following year my father was married. Other members also acquired wives, and still others left Hillcrest. When no bachelors were left, the co-operative ceased to exist.

At about this time my father was promoted to foreman with a pay of three dollars for an eight-hour shift. As an active member of the USDP he was reluctant to accept the position, but the superintendant insisted and his fellow workers also encouraged him to take the job, arguing that it would be better to have their own man in the position than a stranger. After taking a course and being granted a diploma, my father assumed his new responsibilities. There were twenty miners in his team, and he tried to make life easier for them. He would often tell them to lie down and rest when the coal was being mined with the admonition that when the coal-carts descended he would cry out and they would have to get up on their feet to load the coal. The arrangement worked well, and relations remained friendly and harmonious.

The most miraculous event in my father's life was living through the Hillcrest mine disaster, in which almost two hundred people died and only about a dozen survived. It was a terrible tragedy, one of the biggest mine disasters in the world. Yet even in Canada few people know about it.

The morning of 19 June 1914 was bright and beautiful in Hillcrest. The miners were joking and laughing as they collected their safety lamps and descended into the bowels of the earth. "Just before the descent into the mine with the other miners," my father wrote, "the superintendant told me that a new horse had been acquired for my team and it was up to me to break him in and train him in hauling the coal-carts from the shafts to the hoist in the main shaft."

Having reached the bottom of the pit, I went to the horses and had no difficulty in locating the new horse. He stood somewhat aside, trembling with fright. I went to him, patted him, spoke softly into his ear and asked him to be well-mannered because he and I depended on each other and had to be friends. I gave him two cubes of sugar, and the horse calmed down and looked at me with his large, dark eyes. I harnessed him, attached the chain to the six empty coal-carts and, leading the horse by the holster, walked along the tracks while he dragged the empty carts behind him. He did not seem to be afraid and did not try to buck or run.

Coming up to the chute, I found two of my workers ready to load the coal that was collected there. Both walked around the horse, looked at him from all sides and gave their approval. The chute was opened, and the coal came down into the carts. I stood on the bumper of the first cart, holding on to the cart with one hand and with the other holding the Wolff safety lamp, shedding only a meagre light so that the horse could see ahead and would not panic in the darkness. It was very important for the horse to see because stones or coal would often break off from the ceiling and fall on the tracks. Then one had to disconnect the chain and the horse had to be trained to stand still because there were no reins or shaft to guide him. It was important for the horse to be trained to re-spond to verbal commands and not to move too swiftly because otherwise the momentum of the loaded coal-carts would overtake him and injure or even crush him and the driver, in this case me. Should that happen, I always had handy several stout pieces of wood tapered at the ends that could be inserted into the spokes of the cart-wheels, thus braking them. Without too much trouble or fear on the part of the horse, the carts were hauled to the switch, where eight empty carts were then pulled back to the chute or coal face, as the case may be. The boys loaded the carts, each of which, when filled, weighed a ton and a half, and each miner placed his number on the cart containing the coal that he had mined. Again without incident my new horse hauled the carts away to the parking, where I met Superintendant Stewart. "How is the horse behaving?" he asked. I merely pointed at the eight full carts, and he grinned and appeared to be ready to kiss either me or my horse.

This time I decided to collect the coal from the face itself. This was about nine o'clock in the morning. Five carts had been loaded at the face, and I climbed down to see what was the matter with the horse because he was acting strangely, prancing about and being very uneasy. While I was trying to calm him down there was a sudden loud explosion. The ground on which we stood seemed to shake, and the concussion almost burst our eardrums. Some people were knocked off their feet, and some even lost consciousness. Our lamps were extinguished by the rushing air. Anxious cries began to be heard from all sides, inquiring what had happened. Some conjectured that it was a huge cave-in. Others thought that an explosion had occurred. All of a sudden I became aware of the extreme quiet in the mine. There was no sound of ventilation and no movement of air. There were eighty-four miners in that part of the mine. Panic grew. Cries were heard from all sides, cries of fear, pleas for help, cries of pain. I grabbed hold of my horse and shouted to everyone within hearing distance to follow me to the main shaft, believing that the rescue teams would surely come down to find us and bring us to the surface. It became very difficult to breathe, and I found that when I stayed as close to the ground as possible there seemed to be more air to breathe. Soon my horse staggered and then collapsed at the switches. On hands and knees I passed the fallen horse and continued on, urging my fellow workers on as well. Spittle and foam formed around my mouth, and I felt it trickling down my chin. The heat was intense, and both the rails and the ground were hot to the touch. Quite by accident, I came upon an old cross-cut that was sealed off but at one time had led to the outside. Breathing was a little easier now. I urged my friends to come to me because this way lay salvation. Four managed to crawl to me. Other voices were asking for help. I crawled back and managed to pull three more people into the cross-cut before my strength deserted me.

Some hidden reserves of energy came to the fore, compelling us to continue crawling up the slope. Far ahead we saw flames. Again cries of dismay and panic escaped from the throats of the eight of us. Fortunately, the fire was not large. Some coal was burning, and the timber props were also on fire, but they did not prove to be a barrier to our passage.

With our last ounces of strength we crawled and pushed ourselves forward, and just when the tiny light of the opening to the outside was discernible we collapsed out of sheer exhaustion or perhaps because of the sudden abundance of breathable air. When I recovered, I noticed that we were all lying in vomit and some of my friends were still unconscious, but writhing as if in great agony. The eight of us were rescued and helped out into daylight.

The first person who approached me was the manager, Brown, who asked about his brother. I told him that it was very unlikely that anyone had survived in the south shaft. He was overcome with grief. I remember, too, the mine whistle continually blasting, in series of three whistles. This was the signal for an emergency. People from the surrounding mining camps of Coleman, Blairmore, Frank, Belleview, Maple Leaf and Passberg were gathering to render aid. All the while black smoke belched from the mouth of the tunnel.

I saw one of the firebosses lead out six other miners through a shaft along which air had been pumped into the mine. The explosion had wrecked the tracks, but they were soon repaired, and at four o'clock the hoist started letting empty carts down the main tunnel. They were brought up loaded with burned and mangled corpses from the south tunnel. The bodies from the north tunnel were untouched. The miners had merely suffocated.

At the mine entrance there was bedlam as hundreds of

people – wives, children and friends of the miners trapped below – were waiting for news of their loved ones. Even the police could not disperse the people and bring order to the scene. Shops and grocery stores from Hillcrest and the surrounding towns responded by sending sandwiches, drinks and other food. The people stood vigil for three days and two nights at the mine entrance.

The mine manager had asked me to take charge of caring for the bodies. I got the carpenters to build long tables in the washhouse. Volunteers washed the corpses and wrapped them in shrouds cut from huge rolls of linen. The bodies were then transported by wagon to the church, where they were laid out. CPR gangs prepared graves by digging two long parallel trenches. On the third day wooden coffins arrived, and merchants from the whole Crow's Nest Pass lent their delivery wagons to transport the coffins to the cemetery.

The funeral was held on 23 June 1914. The day was cool, and wet snow was falling as endless wagons bore the remains of the miners to their final resting place in the Hillcrest cemetery. I saved three people – M. Fedoruk, Ivan Semotiuk and a friend from the village of Maivtsi. Eight of my friends from my native village died in the explosion.

After this great tragedy the mine was closed. I left Hillcrest for Calgary, but could not find work there and pushed on to Banff. The CPR was building a hotel there and was giving out construction jobs. The fellow hiring crews asked for twenty dollars, and I was not about to part with that much money just to get a job. I thought of returning to the old country, but did not have enough money for a ticket. Ivan Semotiuk, whom I had saved at the mine, in gratitude for his life offered to give me five quarters of an acre of land and waited for me two days in Calgary to try to convince me to take the gift and return home with him. I declined his generous offer, and he went back by himself, only to be recruited by the Austro-

Hungarian authorities when the war broke out to serve as a teamster for the army. Shortly thereafter he was killed by a stray bullet.

I then received a letter that the mine manager wanted me to come back and was offering me a job. I rounded up four friends from my village and took them with me to Hillcrest. The manager told me that he appreciated everything I had done during and after the mine disaster and wanted me to be a boss. I told him that I wanted a job and was prepared to work in the mine, but did not want to be any kind of boss. The manager argued that the work was hard and dangerous. He convinced me, and I became a boss. The work was much easier, and things were going very well.

When the mine in Michelle, British Columbia, was closed because it contained high levels of methane, the superintendant of the mine was transferred to Hillcrest. He was a Welshman. He took a liking to me, and through him I was able to place a number of Ukrainians in various jobs in the Hillcrest mine.

In 1914 the war broke out. There was much agitation to have people join the army. An army camp was constructed in Frank. The recruiting officer from the camp went from hotel to hotel, buying drinks for the miners and trying to get them to sign up. It was hard to stay out of his clutches.

In early 1913, my father received a letter from the Austro-Hungarian authorities ordering him to report for military service in Sniatyn and threatening him with a court-martial if he failed to obey. He decided to apply for Canadian citizenship. He was one of the very few Ukrainians who did so and was severely criticized. The outbreak of the First World War showed that his decision had been the right one. "Enemy aliens," all those who had come to these shores from the multi-national Austro-Hungarian empire, could not acquire Canadian citizenship. Many of the enemy aliens were interned. Others were put into labour battalions that worked on various projects – road building, forestry, railways and so on. They were paid minimal wages, considerably below the prevailing rate.[7] Some people who had acquired citizenship only recently found that it had been revoked. My father's citizenship was not revoked, but he was nonetheless registered as an enemy alien and required to carry an identity card. He described in his autobiography how the enemy aliens were treated:

> When national registration came into effect, everyone had to carry his identity card with him at all times. Of course, only Canadian citizens received registration cards. Germans, Austrians and Ukrainians were rounded up as enemy aliens, and some were interned in camps. Others were put to work building roads for five dollars a month, under the eyes of armed sentries. Discipline was strict, and there were cases where people were hanged for disobedience. Those "former enemy aliens" who had become British subjects and registered nevertheless had to report to the police every month. Some were required to report even two or three times a month. From time to time a mounted policeman would come around, stop people in the hotels and streets and ask them to produce their registration cards. If they could not produce their cards, the policeman would arrest them, handcuff them to a long chain and then, when he had five to ten captives, hook one end of the chain to his saddle and ride off to Frank, forcing the captives to trot along. In Frank, a magistrate would fine them for failing to produce their registration cards. I myself had to pay fines on a number of occasions simply because I had forgotten to take my registration card with me and could not produce it when it was requested. This was a racket.

---

7. For more on this episode in Ukrainian-Canadian history see Lubomyr Y. Luciuk, *A Time for Atonement: Canada's First National Internment Operations and the Ukrainian Canadians 1914-1920* (Kingston: The Limestone Press, 1988).

At this time about seventy-five Ukrainians were employed in various jobs with the Hillcrest Collieries. The new general manager of the mine, Stevenson, liked Ukrainians. Perhaps he only valued them as good workers whom he hated to lose. In any event, he always came to the assistance of any Ukrainian miner who was threatened by the authorities. His attitude did not sit well with the other Anglo-Saxons and the French-Canadians. Secret meetings were held at which we were denounced as enemies, and a resolution was passed demanding ·that Stevenson fire this "undesirable element." He refused. The "loyalist" faction then announced that they were going out on strike and would not work until the "foreigners" had been fired. The mine superintendant asked me to round up all the Ukrainians, regardless of the shift that they worked, and to report for work immediately. Realizing what was at stake, we worked very hard. Sweat ran down our bodies because we had to do the job of two or three men. However, there was no complaining, and everyone worked with will. Our Anglo-Saxon fellow workers looked with open mouths at the way we produced. They were helpless to do anything because this was not a legal strike and we were not scabs. After a week of sitting around and watching us work, they quietly returned to their jobs.

My father was seriously injured in May 1915. He was now a "driver boss," in charge of the teams of men and horses that hauled the coal from the miners to the main shaft, where it was pulled up to the surface by motorized hoists. He was standing between two carts and coupling them together when some carts up ahead came loose and rolled down the track, hitting the carts between which he was standing. His leg was crushed. Dr. Rose, the local general practitioner treated him. Part of the house in which he lived was set aside as a "hospital," and his wife acted as the nurse when he performed surgery. Later, when my father went to hospitals in Europe and Toronto, doctors would look at his leg and marvel.

"What surgeon performed this operation?" they would ask. Rose at first wanted to amputate the leg, but my father said, "No, I'd rather die than have my leg amputated, because what am I worth with only one leg?" So Rose, who had never performed such a procedure, took out a textbook, studied the description and illustrations and then kept looking at the book while he operated. He used surgical nails (which cost seventy-five dollars, my father noted in his account book) to fasten the top part of the leg to the pelvis. After he recovered from the injury, my father got a topside job. As the men on each shift finished their work and came out they would hand in their lamps and my father would charge them up and then hand out charged lamps to the men going down on the next shift.

CHAPTER 2

CHILDHOOD

Until the First World War broke out, my father thought that he would go back and marry a girl in the "old country." He even sent money to his family to buy land in his name for the day he would come home. When the war ended and it was possible to go to Ukraine again, however, my father concluded that he was getting on in years and should settle down. There was nothing romantic about his decision. Once he had decided to get married, the question was, to whom? There were very few single Ukrainian women in Hillcrest or in the mining camps. So he turned to a friend named Kuzyk from Karliv, who had chosen to farm in northern Alberta. "Are there any marriageable women in your area?" my father wrote. "Oh yes, quite a few," Kuzyk replied. "Come on up and I will look after you." My father bought a car and drove to Lanuke, which was later renamed Two Hills. It took him two weeks to get to his destination, he once told me. The maximum speed was thirty miles an hour, but he had to travel at ten or twenty miles an hour because the roads were so poor. The car would often get stuck in the mud, and my father would have to go to the nearest house to get a farmer with a team of horses to pull him out. He was certainly the centre of attraction when he finally arrived. Many people in Lanuke had never seen a car. Here was a rich man with lots of money and a car. My father looked one or two women over, found my mother, looked her over and asked, "Will you be my wife?" She was seventeen at the time. He was thirty-one.

My mother Maria was living at home with her parents, an older brother and sister and two younger sisters. Her parents, Vasyl and Varvara Nykyforuk, had immigrated to Canada at the turn of the century and settled on a 160-acre homestead that they bought for ten dollars near Lanuke. They came from the village of Kniazhe on the border of the Pokuttia region. The village still has that

29

name. It is situated on the river Cheremosh, which under Austro-Hungarian rule formed the boundary between the provinces of Galicia and Bukovyna and in the inter-war years delineated the border between Poland and Romania. My grandmother married my grandfather, who was then a thirty-year-old widower, at the age of fifteen. They had one or two children in Ukraine. The rest were born in Canada. My mother was born in 1902.

My father asked Maria's father for his consent. Vasyl Nykyforuk looked at my father, said that he would have to pay all the wedding expenses and gave his permission. Although this was a Ukrainian settlement, there was no Ukrainian Orthodox or Catholic priest. But there was a Ukrainian Presbyterian minister, the Reverend Perich, who was my wife's mother's brother-in-law because he had married her oldest sister. Thus my future wife's uncle by marriage married my parents. And so my parents were married in a Ukrainian Presbyterian church. The wedding lasted a week: people ate, drank, went to sleep, got up and ate and drank again. When the celebration was over, my parents drove to Hillcrest. The marriage was almost like the proxy marriages that some people still arrange. There was no love or romance in it. My father had weighed whatever had to be weighed and had made his decision. As it turned out, it was not much of a marriage, and they were separated after a quarter of a century. There were two children, my brother Michael, who was born in 1923, and I.

I have many photographs from my father, all very good even after the passage of time. They were taken by Thomas Gushul, an extraordinary photographer from Blairmore, a mining town slightly larger than Frank or Hillcrest, several miles west of Frank along the highway to British Columbia. Gushul's house, which was still standing when I went to the Crow's Nest Pass several years ago, was a wooden structure covered with weathered shingles and with a number of windows in the roof and walls. I remember those windows very clearly because I went there on several occasions to have family pictures taken. Gushul, who had come to Canada from the province of Bukovyna, had rigged curtains with strings and rods so that he could control the amount of light coming through the windows. He didn't merely wait for people to come to him, but would pack up his equipment and go from camp to camp, photographing celebrations and family events. The photographs he took sixty or seventy years ago are still in excellent condition. Some look as if they were taken a week ago. I've often thought that it would be important to get hold of Gushul's negatives because they record the early history of the region.

I was born on 7 July 1920. My father celebrated by throwing a shindig. The Presbyterian minister, the only clergyman in the town, christened me. Gushul came to record the event, and I have a photograph of all the guests in front of our house – the entire Ukrainian community of Hillcrest as well as people from the neighbouring towns of Belleview, Frank, Blairmore and Coleman.

My birth certificate gave my surname as "Wasyl Frolak." Not knowing the Cyrillic alphabet, Canadian immigration officers of ten spelled an immigrant's name phonetically, distorting it considerably. My father had his name written in various ways. It was unheard of in those days not to anglicize one's non-English name. Thus every Vasyl became William; Moishe became Morris, and Czeslaw became Chester. My parents and their Ukrainian friends called me Vasyl. Outside the home, I was Bill.

When I went to Western Ukraine and enrolled at a *gymnasium* in Stanyslaviv, I was required to produce a certificate of baptism, because that was more important in a Catholic country than a birth certificate. Under Polish rule, there was no separation of church and state, and religion was a compulsory subject in all the schools. You were not excused for not being a Catholic or, for that matter, a Christian.

Since I could not produce a baptismal certificate, I had to confess that I had not been baptized. This created a serious problem. Together with Koch, a Jewish classmate, I was relegated to the back of the room in the religion class. We could neither participate in the class nor leave. I don't know what grade Koch received, but my rating was only "fair." I was probably the only one who received such a low grade. Religion was the easiest subject, and everyone received a grade of "very good." And so when I was sixteen or seventeen I decided to be baptized in a proper Catholic ceremony. In honour of that occasion I was given a "Christian" name, Sviatoslav.

I was baptized in the chapel of the *bursa*, or residence, at the *gymnasium*. The priest who taught catechism officiated at the baptism, and my mathematics teacher was my godfather. My landlady, Mrs. Hanushevsky, at whose home in the suburb of Uhornyky I was living, was my godmother. Later my brother went through the same process. I think that I am probably the only person who is his own brother's godfather.

When I came back to Canada in 1941 and enrolled in medicine at the University of Toronto, I gave my first name as Sviatoslav. The professors, the lab people and my fellow students all looked at the name and took a run at pronouncing it, but with no success. Even my friends didn't know what to call me. They called me "Mac," "George," "Chief," anything but Sviatoslav. After a year or two I decided that I was not going to respond to "Hey, Uke!" all my life and adopted the name Stanley.

Still another change in my name occurred after the war, when I was thinking of running for office and decided to spell my surname as "Frolick," which is easier to pronounce and more closely approximates the Ukrainian pronunciation and the original German "Fröhlich" of my great-great-grandfather.

In Hillcrest in the early 1920s there were between fifty and a hundred Ukrainians. They were miners, but they had brought a high level of national awareness with them from Pokuttia. The first leaders of the Ukrainian settlers in Canada – Petro Zvarych, Myroslav Stechishin, Taras Ferley, Ivan Bodrug, Yaroslav Arsenych, Roman Kremar and Kyrylo Genyk, who as an immigration officer and CPR agent helped carry out the grand colonization scheme of Joseph Oleskiw – came almost exclusively from Pokuttia. Dedicated to socialism, they sought to implant it among their countrymen in the form of Ukrainian branches of the Socialist Party of Canada, which subsequently transformed themselves into the independent Ukrainian Social Democratic Party. Such socialist organizers as Ivan Bodrug and Pavlo Krat (or Paul Crath, as he spelled his name in English) found fertile soil in the mining camps of Alberta. Even before I was born, Bodrug and

Crath had established a branch of the Ukrainian Social Democratic Party. Crath was an extraordinary man, idealistic and dedicated to his beliefs. He was active in the *Hromada*, the community of Ukrainian expatriates in Saint Petersburg, and took part in the revolution of 1905. After the failure of the revolution, many of them had to emigrate. Crath went to Galicia and then to Canada.

My father said that Crath took up the cause of social democracy with great zeal. He'd go on foot from camp to camp, in all kinds of weather, preaching his political gospel and organizing branches of the USDP. He was also the compiler of the first Ukrainian-English dictionary published in Canada, a pocket-size book in a red cover. At the end there were phrases, such as "Do you have a job?" and "I would like some tea, please," that a person who had just got off the boat could memorize and use. Like Mao's little red book in another age and place, it was ever present as an indispensable aid to our immigrants.

My father was the president of the Hillcrest chapter of the USDP, which had about twenty members. The revolution of 1917 had a profound effect on the Ukrainian socialist movement. The Bolsheviks seized power in Saint Petersburg; the Central Rada in Kiev proclaimed first the autonomy and then the complete independence of Ukraine. These events divided loyalties. The rank and file of the USDP was not sufficiently educated to appreciate what was happening in Ukraine – the struggle for power first in the Central Rada under Mykhailo Hrushevsky, then in the Hetmanate under Pavlo Skoropadsky, and then in the Directorate under Symon Petliura – or to take sides between the Mensheviks and the Bolsheviks. But the leaders certainly did. The cleavage took place at the top and then went down to the bottom. Bodrug and Krat transferred their missionary zeal to religion and were ordained as ministers in the Ukrainian Presbyterian Church. Matthew Shatulsky and John Navizivsky became Communists. Stechishin, Arsenych, Zvarych and Ferley stayed in the nationalist camp and helped shape the institutions of present-day Ukrainian-Canadian life.

In addition to the social and economic aims that it shared with other socialists, the USDP was formally committed to national liberation and the establishment of a sovereign Ukrainian state. The demise of the USDP can therefore be attributed to the defeat of those hopes by the imposition of Communist rule over much of Ukraine. The Bolshevik victory sounded the deathknell for social democrats and indeed all socialists, and the foreign limbs withered away when they were severed from the native trunk.

After 1918 there was no organized Ukrainian life in Hillcrest because neither of the two social-democratic factions could support it. Before that the Ukrainians had had a hall of their own, run by the USDP, which was only two doors away from our house. Now it is converted into a garage. They had also hired a man named Berkosha, who had completed *gymnasium* in Western Ukraine, to teach their children Ukrainian after hours, and each member of the USDP executive contributed out of his own pocket to pay Berkosha's salary and to put on plays. You can imagine the quality of the performances with the limited talent available. I have a picture of my father's, from 1912 or so, of carollers, four men dressed as shepherds. Their costumes were pitiful, and instead of shepherds' crooks they carried tree branches, but they bore a *vertep*, a nativity scene with a star on top.

By the time I was born, the Ukrainian school had been closed, but my father taught my brother and me to read and write Ukrainian. My mother, who grew up in a Ukrainian block settlement in north-east Alberta where Ukrainian was the only language of communication, still speaks English with an accent. The teacher at her public school was a Ukrainian and although he taught in English, he spoke it with an accent. This was after bilingual Ukrainian schools were abolished in Alberta and Ukrainian teachers lost their teaching certificates. A long struggle between the Ukrainians and other settlers on one side and the provincial education authorities on the other ensued. It had all sorts of political and social repercussions for Western Canada. To teach the children Ukrainian after normal school hours, local school boards hired teachers, and the communities made sure they knew Ukrainian. Many teachers merely went through the motions of teaching in English and thus nominally conforming to the laws of the province. In my mother's school, for example, the teacher taught in Ukrainian more than in English. So the children didn't get much of an English education. My mother recalls that her teacher would always keep an eye on the window. If a stranger appeared in the yard, he would say to the children, "Hide your Ukrainian readers and get out your English readers," and then watch to make sure that the stranger did not turn out to be an inspector from the provincial department of education.

I cannot recall whether my father read any Ukrainian newspapers, but I remember that there were Ukrainian books and phonograph records in the house. My father also subscribed to children's magazines from Western Ukraine, one of which was *Dzvinochok*, "The Little Bell." Once he submitted a picture of me on skis and my brother on a sled, with a donation of a dollar or two. I was very impressed when the issue with my photograph arrived. There was my picture in a magazine from far-away Europe! My father was adamant that we learn to read Ukrainian, and since no educational material in Ukrainian was produced in this country, he ordered children's books from Lviv, the capital of Western Ukraine. There were translations of Aesop, Grimm and Anderson, Ukrainian classics like Ivan Franko's *Lys Mykyta*, or "Fox Mykyta," and readers. They referred to things that were completely beyond our experience – pictures of whitewashed houses with storks nesting on the thatched roofs, for example. "What are those birds?" I would ask my father. "Storks," he would explain. Who had ever seen a stork in Hillcrest? There were pictures of barefoot children grazing geese on the common. We didn't know what a common was and had never seen geese being grazed. And there were references to hedgehogs. We had seen porcupines, but hedgehogs were unfamiliar to us.

My father did not want us to lose our identity or to forget Ukrainian. Of course, we spoke not standard Ukrainian, but the Pokuttia dialect, an example of which can be found in the writings of Vasyl Stefanyk. Every night my father gave us lessons in reading and writing, to which we strenuously objected, but to no avail. And when we we got bored or tired, he would read to us. He read to us the way other people read a chapter of the Bible every evening. To prevent us from forgetting Ukrainian, my father also did not permit my brother and me to associate with other children. Our contact with them was through the fence, and I played only with my brother.

As a consequence, when I started public school at the age of six in September 1926, I did not know a word of English. I came home from my first day at school in tears because I had not been able to tell the teacher that I had to go to the toilet. I suppose that the Ukrainian children in the class could have helped out, but how can you expect a six-year-old to act as an interpreter? So I wet my pants. The teacher sent me home. I felt very hard done by because I had tried to tell her that I had to go to the toilet and she hadn't understood me. I came home crying and vowing that I would never go back to school.

Despite my initial difficulties at school, I soon became a good pupil and stood at the top of my class until I completed grade six and we departed for Europe. My one weakness was talking in class, and my teachers often wrote, "Wasyl talks too much," on my report cards.

The public school in Hillcrest was not like a country school, where all the children sit together in one room. There were separate rooms and a separate teacher for each grade. I suspect that Hillcrest Collieries, the company that owned the mines in the Pass, contributed a goodly portion of the school budget. The company was quite benevolent. Although Hillcrest was not a company town in the usual sense – houses were privately owned – the company did provide all the services and utilities, including running water and electricity, without cost. Aside from a few people employed as store clerks, all the wage earners worked for the company. The social life in the community revolved around the home, the church and the mine workers' union, which occasionally staged cultural and social events in its hall.

When I started school, my father insisted that I also go to church. Although he was fiercely anti-clerical and agnostic, like all the Ukrainian radical socialists of his time, he thought that the church might instill some ethics in me. I grew up as a regular churchgoer in the United Church, attending Sunday school and evening services every week. There was no other church in

Hillcrest. Just before we left Canada, a Roman Catholic church was built. I was in it only twice: to take part in a funeral and to attend a wedding. Sometimes my mother would go to church with my brother and me, but my father never did, probably because he was embarrassed by his poor English.

At first I went to Sunday school because my father made me go, but I soon began to like it. I became the pastor's pet and took pleasure in my exalted position. Early on Sunday morning I would get the key to the church at the pastor's house, then go to the church, take the hymnals out of the back cupboard and put them out in the pews. After making sure that everything was in order I would ring the bells in the belfry.

The United Church encouraged children to attend Sunday school by giving them religious pictures. Noah's ark was one such inducement. Every attendance earned a stamp-like picture of a different pair of animals. We would lick the backs and paste them into the blank space on the picture. If attendance was perfect, the whole picture would eventually be filled. If not, blank spaces would stick out like sore thumbs, rendering the picture incomplete and useless. This was superior to collecting gopher tails or baseball cards.

Like my father, I am anti-clerical, because I don't like the way priests dominate organized Ukrainian life, from the Ukrainian Canadian Committee to the World Congress of Free Ukrainians. At conventions and congresses the priests sit in the front row like blackbirds on a rail, acting as if they were the font of wisdom and telling lay people what resolutions to pass and whom to elect to the governing bodies. Do they think we are still in the eighteenth century, when there was no middle class or intelligentsia and when the Ukrainian nation, as the Poles scornfully declared, consisted only of *chlop i pop*, or peasant and priest? It's still the peasant and priest, with the latter sitting in the place of honour and telling the former what to do. What right do the priests have to meddle in lay organizations? Would they stand for it if I attended their synods and told them how to run their ecclesiastical affairs? Yet they order members of their lay organizations whom to elect to the executive body. I consider this attitude insulting because it presupposes that the priests know what is best for the community. "A shoemaker should stick to his last," a Ukrainian proverb says.

I became aware of prejudice for the first time in 1930, when I was ten years old and travelled with my mother and brother to Vancouver to visit my aunt and her family. Now you can travel by rail, but in those days there was no direct route from Hillcrest to Vancouver. The train went as far as the head of the Kootenay Lakes, where you had to detrain, get on a ferry, sail up the chain of lakes, get off the ferry and then continue your journey by rail. The Doukhobors had large settlements around the Kootenay Lakes and in the foothills of the Rockies, and when they came to Hillcrest to sell their produce, they often stayed at our place. They were fine people, very religious and industrious.

On this trip up the Kootenay Lakes, which was on a Sunday, the Doukhobor passengers assembled on the deck to hold a service and sing hymns. I had never heard a choir before as there was no choir in Hillcrest and I was very impressed by the Doukhobors' beautiful singing. Suddenly the ferry crew ran up on deck and shouted at them to stop. The Doukhobors kept on singing. Then the crew got rough and started pushing them about to make them disperse. As a ten-year-old, I couldn't understand why the ferry crew treated the Doukhobors that way. They were very nice people, weren't bothering anyone and were singing beautifully. That was my first experience with what I later came to know as racism.

Perhaps because the town was small and all the working men belonged to the same union, the discrimination was less visible in Hillcrest, and there were few racial or ethnic problems. Nonetheless, everyone took it for granted that there were two classes: the ruling Anglo-Saxons and the immigrants. My father was a boss, but a small one, and the big bosses, as well as the doctor, the minister, the bank manager, the postmaster and most of the teachers, were English. Except for a Slovak who had a grocery store, two Chinese, one of whom ran a cafe and the other a grocery store, and a Syrian who owned a dry-goods store, the merchants were also English. Although people did not live in isolation and visited their neighbours for coffee or tea, there was an invisible barrier between the English and the rest of the people that could never be crossed. Halloween was the only time in the year when we children were allowed to visit the home of Mr. Stevenson, the mine superintendent. We had to use the back door and could go only into the kitchen or on the porch. The Stevensons would have apples floating in a tub of water. We would be given kitchen forks and told to drop them from the level of our chests. If the fork speared an apple, it was ours. If the fork missed – tough luck!

My father was a judicious disciplinarian. This made the punishment he meted out impersonal, but did not help my brother and me to bear the pain and humiliation. We knew that we would be punished for any transgression – coming home late from school, for example – and tried to make pacts for mutual assistance. If my brother was going to get a licking, I would plead with my father not to punish him. If my entreaties fell on deaf ears, I'd grab his arm and try to keep the blow from coming down on my brother's vulnerable backside. Occasionally this worked, but for the most part it didn't. Sometimes my mother would intercede for us, with mixed results.

My father kept a switch in the kitchen, and when it became dry and stiff, part of our punishment would be to bring a fresh one. I hated that part more the punishment itself. Can you imagine not only being beaten, but having to go out and get the tool? When I say my father was judicious, I mean that he played the role of a judge. He wouldn't yell or cuff us, and I don't think he ever hit us in anger. He'd make the charge known and then pass sentence. "You're going to get two" – or three or four, whatever the sentence was – "blows of this switch across your bottom." Then he would ceremoniously pull a chair into the middle of the kitchen and tell us to bend over and expose our backsides. As he hit us, he would count the strokes until the sentence was carried out. Then he would demand that we thank him for "the lesson." That was particularly humiliating. I would have preferred two or three more strokes of the switch to having to thank him for being punished.

Although I may have pictured Hillcrest as a backwater where nothing happened, that is not entirely the case. In 1926 or 1927,

Walter Moser, an immigrant from Switzerland who had settled in Hillcrest, conceived the idea of organizing a symphony orchestra. Long before orchestras existed in Edmonton or Calgary, the remote mining community of Hillcrest had the first symphony orchestra in Alberta. It was not a professional orchestra – the people played for the love of music and were not paid – but they did go from place to place, giving concerts and performances.

My father could not distinguish one note from another, and I don't remember him singing even in the bathtub, but he loved music, and we had a phonograph – rather a rarity in the 1920s – and records of Caruso. My father wanted to give me a musical education, and under duress I studied the violin with Moser. I practiced every day for half an hour and went to Moser's house once a week for half-hour lessons, which cost, as I remember, a dollar and a half, a lot of money in those days. Once a year representatives of the Royal Conservatory of Music in Toronto would come to Crow's Nest Pass; local adjudicators would be appointed, and musical festivals would be held at which students, most of them Moser's, would perform. At home we had a clock under a glass dome with balls turning first one way and then the other. I remember it clearly because I glued my eyes to it while I was playing to make sure that I did not practice a minute more than the obligatory half an hour. Needless to say, I did not set the world on fire with my musical talent. When I left for Ukraine, my father insisted that I take my violin along and made me promise to practice faithfully, but when I arrived at my uncle's house I put the violin away in a cupboard and never picked it up again.

Ukrainian immigrants in Canada placed great emphasis on musical education. As far as I was able to observe, there was no such emphasis in the old country. At the *gymnasium*s that I attended there was choir practice, but solo singing and instrument playing were not available. I still don't understand why the same people, once they had moved to Canada, should have valued music so highly. Even the earliest Ukrainian-Canadian organizations had choirs and orchestras. Unable to afford brass bands or symphonies, they chose inexpensive instruments. In north-east Alberta, for example, mandolin orchestras were very popular with

Ukrainian organizations and even served to recruit members. My mother was taught to play the mandolin when she went to school, and her school had an orchestra as early as 1910. Musical activities were an integral part of growing up in the Ukrainian community in western Canada.

Women were not wage earners, but they cooked, cleaned and washed clothes. Most people in Hillcrest had a vegetable garden. We kept chickens for their eggs and meat and cows for their milk, butter, cheese and manure. Our small garden was well fertilized with the output from two cows. We started out with one cow and had much more milk than we needed, so we sold it to our neighbours. This business was so successful that we got a second cow. My father helped my mother to milk the cows, and my brother and I, much to our disgust, would come home from school and instead of going out to play deliver milk to our customers. We could only take three or four quarts in the bottle carrier. For a seven- or eight-year-old that was a big load and a long distance.

The cows were my mother's business. All the money from the milk went into her own bank account. She insisted on that. Over the years the money grew into a tidy sum. Later my father conceived the idea that we would go carolling on Christmas Eve and Christmas Day, which in the Julian calendar fall on 6 and 7 January. He taught us two carols. I was not much of a singer, and my brother wasn't much better, but to our parents' surprise, and to our own great pleasure, we were received warmly wherever we went. No one had ever gone carolling from house to house in Hillcrest. The nostalgia for the native country that was evoked by two children singing Christmas carols often brought tears to the people's eyes and hugs and kisses for us. More gratifying to my father was that people showed their appreciation by rewarding us with a dollar or two. My father loved money, and from then until we left Hillcrest we carolled to the religious, the atheists and the agnostics in our community.

Since the observance of the Ukrainian Christmas tradition had proved to be so rewarding, my father decided to use Easter for the same end and had my mother paint *pysanky*, or Easter eggs. She would be busy with the wax and the dyes day and night, painting dozens of eggs, and my brother and I would trundle the *pysanky* from door to door. They were an even bigger hit with both the Ukrainian and the non-Ukrainian families in Hillcrest than the Christmas carols, and the money they brought was added to the money in my mother's account.

A thrifty man who thought that spending money was almost sinful, my father would not allow my brother and me to keep any of the money from the carolling or the sale of the Easter eggs. We did well if we got a five-cent ice-cream cone and a dime for the cinema once a month. When we grew out of our shoes we had to wear them and suffer. You couldn't throw shoes away merely because they had become tight. As a result, my toes are permanently deformed.

I left Hillcrest when I was twelve and came back when I was twenty-one. I couldn't get over how different the reality was from my childhood recollections. Everything appeared so near, so small, so shrunken! When we lived in Hillcrest, the school seemed to be miles away. Now it was a stone's throw away. When I was a child, I thought that delivering milk was very onerous because I measured distances by a child's footsteps. Now as an adult I saw distances in a completely different perspective.

CHAPTER 3

JOURNEY TO UKRAINE

My father made many promises, few of which he kept. A child is a trusting soul. It dreams about the fulfilment of promises given, and when the promises are broken, so is the child's heart. I vowed that when I had children of my own, I would never make a promise I could not keep. I suppose that my mother felt the same way because my father made promises to her, too, one of which was a trip to Ukraine. "Promises, promises," my mother said. "Everything is going well," my father replied. "We're making money. Why spend it?" My mother, usually docile and pliable, was adamant. She had concluded that she had milked the cows long enough and deserved a holiday.

In 1932, when I was twelve years old, my father finally gave in and bought return tickets to the village of Tatariv in the Carpathian Mountains of Western Ukraine for my mother, my brother and me out of the milk, Easter egg and carolling fund. The tickets were valid for six months. The company would not let my father leave for six months, and so my mother, my brother and I packed our trunks and boarded a train (which was held up for us because we were late in getting to the station). Half the town came to see us off because no one had ever gone to Ukraine on a holiday. People left only when they had saved enough money to return to their native villages for the rest of their lives.

Off we went! By train to Montreal, where we boarded the *SS Montcalm*, a passenger liner of the Cunard White Star Line bound for Southampton and Le Havre. As luck would have it, only days out of Canada my brother and I came down with chicken pox and were quarantined in the ship's hospital. When we landed in France, an ambulance took us straight from the dock to a hospital run by French nuns, none of whom spoke English. My mother, who spoke no French and had never been further away from home than Vancouver, somehow found accommodations for herself in the city. Eventually she persuaded the hospital authorities to give her a bed so that she could be with us in the ward. We were very happy because now we had another person to talk to.

Like prisons, hospitals are always depressing, but the one in Le Havre was especially so, both because we couldn't communicate with anyone and because the windows were painted over with white paint, like the windows in the church in Hillcrest, to keep the patients from being distracted while they were recovering. At the top of the arch in each window was a transom with clear glass, but the view was far from enchanting: a road that went up a hill and funeral hearses that drove to a cemetery at the top.

The food was terrible. For breakfast we got a watery gruel with prunes in it. Lunch and dinner were no better. At first my mother went out and bought fruit for us, but the nuns soon gave her to understand that this was not permissible, and we were left completely dependent on the hospital fare. The beds also presented a problem. It was probably a French custom to take away the pillows we used all day and to replace them with cylindrical rolls. They were not as hard as Chinese or Japanese headrests, but I couldn't go to sleep, and the nights were long and miserable. To this day I shudder when I think about that hospital: I cannot say a single positive thing about it.

I have no recollections of the trip across France and Germany to Poznan in Poland. The first thing I remember was being awakened at night by Polish custom officials. My mother was nervous because she was carrying twenty of the twenty-five-dollar American gold coins known as gold eagles. Happily, the officials found nothing amiss.

The next day is still vivid in my mind. It was morning, the sun was shining brightly, and my nose was pressed against the window as I tried to get a closer look at the country that was our destination. Somewhere in this country of Poland was *Halychyna*, Galicia, Western Ukraine, the land whence my ancestors had come. Would it look like what I could see from the train?

It's surprising what insignificant things make enough of an impression to stay in your memory. I remember how puzzled I was when I saw peasants travelling along the road in their wagons. They were quite different from Canadian wagons, which were box-like and big. Here they were much smaller and shaped like a trough, and the harnesses were different.

As the rural scenes outside seemed to be unchanging, tedium soon set in, and Mike and I looked for ways to pass the time. My mother had brought along my stamp album, and when my brother and I began to look through the collection, a passenger in our compartment took an album out of his bag, showed his stamps to us and then looked mine over. In the end he gave me a number of stamps I did not have. I was pleased to have them and thought that the stranger was a very nice man.

Our destination was the railway station at Tatariv. My uncle lived eight miles away in the village of Yablonytsia in the Chornohora, or Black Mountain, range of the Carpathians and was in charge of a parish that consisted of three villages, Yablonytsia, Polianytsia Popovychivska and Voronienka, on the border between Poland and Czechoslovakia. Voronienka was the last village on the Polish side, and Yasinnia the first village on the Czechoslovak side. Yet both villages were Ukrainian, and Ukrainians inhabited both Western Ukraine under Polish rule and Carpatho-Ukraine under Czechoslovak domination.

By a strange coincidence, I had come thousands of miles from one mountain pass, the Crow's Nest Pass in the Rockies, to another, the Tatar Pass, in the Carpathians. It was called that because people believed that Kublai Khan's nephew led the Tatar hordes from Asia across the Ukrainian steppes and through the pass and then across the Hungarian plains to lay siege to Vienna.

My father had written to his brother that we were coming to stay with him. After being graduated from university and working as a lawyer, Vasyl had become a celibate Ukrainian Catholic (or Uniate) priest. Not wanting his brother to be critical of us, my father briefed us on religious matters. "You'll have to learn how to cross yourselves," he said, "because your uncle will expect that of you." And he taught us how to make the sign of the cross and to say, in Ukrainian, "In the name of the Father and of the Son and of the Holy Spirit, Amen," and the Lord's Prayer.

No one greeted us when we arrived at the station, perhaps because we had come later than we were supposed to. But there were *calèches*, and my mother went over to ask whether they would take us to Yablonytsia and how much the fare would be. Eventually we got all our baggage on to a *calèche* and drove off. It was dark when we arrived at the manse. My uncle was there, dressed in a black cassock with a stiff Roman collar. Priests always wore cassocks then. I don't remember seeing a priest in Western Ukraine dressed only in slacks and a shirt. I thought that was wonderful because I had never seen a person dressed this way.

The morning after our arrival my uncle announced that we would go to church and he would offer a mass of thanksgiving for our safe arrival. The church was unlike any I had ever seen. The church in Hillcrest had no icons or ornamentation. Here the church was a beautiful wooden structure, built in the traditional style of the Hutsuls, the mountain people of the eastern Carpathians, who are more developed artistically than the people in any other region of Ukraine.

When we walked into the church, we lit the candles in the huge chandelier and then sat down in the pew. In Orthodox and Uniate churches there is only one pew for the cantor, and people stand during the service, men on the right, women on the left. Class distinctions were observed in the church, too, because the family of the priest and distinguished visitors did not have to stand in the main nave with the common folk, but went to the sacristy, from which they had a full view of the altar and could follow the liturgy without being observed by the rest of the congregation.

On this occasion, as we were the only ones in the church, we sat in the cantor's pew. An Orthodox or Uniate church, for a person who is attending it for the first time, is a fantasy. The incense, the flickering candles, the gleaming gilt of the icons and iconostasis and the gold vestments in which my uncle emerged – how different it all was from the austere and uninspired Protestant services to which I was accustomed!

I soon determined that I, too, would be a priest, and for a time I was religious to the point of fanaticism. I went to mass every morning, and on the way to school I would invariably stop in at a

Polish church to say a prayer. This lasted only a year or two, and then politics claimed my allegiance.

My uncle was a complete stranger to me, especially because he was a priest, beyond my reach, on a higher and different plane. Later we became closer, and he often played and wrestled with Mike and me. When we were growing up in Hillcrest, my mother was detached and unemotional. My mother's youngest sister, who is only six years older than I am, told me once, "Our mother never hugged, kissed or cuddled your mother or me. And in turn we didn't do that." I don't remember my mother ever taking me in her arms and kissing me. But my father often played with us. He would pretend to be a wolf or a bear and would chase us, making horrible growling noises. We'd run through the house, shrieking, and hide under the bed. Then he'd pretend that he was pawing to get at us, driving us into a frenzy. We were frightened to the depths of our souls, and at the same time we were thrilled, knowing it was all make-believe.

Unlike my father, my uncle never scolded or punished my brother and me. He played with us, though not as much as my father, but always maintained a distance. He was a priest and as such more than a mere mortal. Yet I loved, admired and respected him, more even than my own father. At first my uncle was a substitute father, but even when my father joined us two years later, I still liked him more. Yet we never confided in each other. Only when the Communists came and everything suddenly turned topsy-turvy – shortages, oppression, much worse than the Polish oppression, people exiled to Siberia, their families never told what had happened to them – did he and I become closer.

In Poland the class distinction between the intelligentsia and the peasants was far more pronounced than the one between the landed gentry and the tenant farmers in England. Age differences were also important. At the *gymnasium* we addressed our classmates by the familiar form *ty*, or "thou." But if they were two classes higher, we used the formal pronoun *vy*, or "you," while they used *ty* to us. Two years made a difference in the relationship. The peasants in the villages held students in high esteem. A *gymnasium* student might be only eleven or twelve years old, but they respected him as an educated person, a potential leader. Similarly, a person who had completed his education and achieved his position in life would treat a student as a lesser being until he had passed his *matura*, or final examination, and had been graduated from the *gymnasium*. My own relationship with my uncle changed drastically after my *matura*. Intimacy was now possible because a degree of equality between us had been reached. It was a warm and good relationship. But of course it was of very short duration.

Because we were the family of the priest all the villagers treated us with deference. Although I was only twelve years old, they didn't call me by my first name, but referred to me as *panych*, or "young master." They kissed my mother's hand, just as they kissed the priest's hand. She had never had her hand kissed. My uncle had two servants, a housekeeper and a manservant who looked after the farm. Later my mother took over the house-keeping, and a maid was hired to replace the housekeeper. By the standards of the village, my uncle was well-to-do. Like every priest, he received a monthly salary from the government for keeping records of births, marriages and deaths and collected fees for performing marriages, baptisms and funerals. Each parish had ecclesiastical lands, and my uncle had more land than the richest person in the village.

The soil in the Carpathians was not very fertile, but it was possible to grow hay, oats and vegetables. Hay was the main crop, and the Hutsuls used it to feed pigs, cows, horses and oxen. In the Podillia region grain was the main crop. In the Pokuttia region, in the foothills of the Carpathians, the staple food was *mamalyga*, or cornmeal mush. And in the Carpathians, boiled potatoes and *bryndzia*, or sheep's cheese, were the staples. Every Hutsul house had a dish of boiled and peeled potatoes next to a dish of salty *bryndzia*. Hospitality dictated that these dishes be offered to everyone who entered the house. There was a ritual to the eating of the food. You took a potato from the plate, broke off a piece and held it in your fist. With the thumb of your other hand you scooped up some of the cheese, pressed it into the potato and then carried the food to your mouth.

Sheepherding was the chief occupation and provided wool, meat, milk and cheese. In the spring the Hutsuls would bring their sheep together and drive the huge herds up into the mountain meadows, where they would stay all summer. In the fall the shepherds would drive the sheep down into the lowlands.

What most impressed us was the country itself. The Rocky Mountains are stark and foreboding. The Carpathians are soft, warm and verdant, with alpine meadows and a profusion of grasses, flowers and juniper bushes. In the lowlands the houses were built in rows along streets. Here in the mountains the houses were scattered. You would see a house here in the valley, a house there on a summit and a house over there by the pine forest.

The people went about on small, wiry mountain ponies. The saddles were carved from oak. The Hutsuls' dress was also colourful. The men wore red woollen pants, embroidered linen shirts, tooled leather belts and sleeveless sheepskin jackets decorated with beads and sequins. In the winter they wore short, heavy woollen coats over the jackets and sheepskin hats. On their feet both men and women wore tooled leather slippers and heavy woollen socks embroidered at the top. The women wore long linen dresses and woollen panels embroidered with metallic threads, all held in place by elaborately embroidered cloth belts. When they rode down on their horses to the church on Sundays and feast-days, the Hutsuls were so colourful that they seemed unreal. All these things – the feeling of belonging, of being among your own, the beautiful environment, the lifestyle, in many ways preferable to what we had known in Canada – contributed to our decision to stay.

My mother made the decision. For the first time since her marriage she was free of my father's domination. And she must have had that sense of contentment and happiness that comes from being in one's own country, with one's own people. Hillcrest was a heterogeneous collection of people who came from different backgrounds and spoke various languages. Here everyone dressed alike, spoke the same language and worshipped alike.

So my mother decided – and if I had been asked I would have concurred – that we would stay here. My mother wrote to my father and said, "You've worked long and hard enough in the coal mine in Hillcrest. We've got enough money. Why don't you come back here? Let's live out our lives here." He kept refusing, and she kept urging him. Six months went by, and we didn't go back.

My uncle had a part in the decision. A month or two after our arrival he said that it was unseemly for my brother and me to be idle. "They should get schooling and not waste their time in idleness," he said. My mother agreed. I don't know why we weren't enrolled in the local school, perhaps because we weren't qualified and would have had to go down a grade or two. I had completed grade six and normally would have been entitled to start *gymnasium*, but my Ukrainian consisted of no more than five hundred fractured words, and my Polish and German were non-existent. "We'll get a good governess and have her teach the boys their lessons," my uncle announced.

Eventually a young lady named Nusia Rovenchuk arrived and began to teach us every day, except Sunday, from morning until five in the afternoon. For a year she taught me Ukrainian, Polish, German, history, geography and all the other subjects that I needed to gain admission to *gymnasium*. She had been graduated from a teaching seminary, but couldn't get a job because teaching was a government position and the Poles were reluctant to hire Ukrainians, especially those active in the national movement. Rovenchuk was a fervid nationalist, perhaps even a member of the OUN, and expounded her views to us without compunction. She had a knack for making Ukrainian history come alive and was probably one of the best teachers I ever had. I became what I am primarily because of her.

My uncle, by contrast, was a patriot but not a nationalist. During the war he served in the Austrian army as a second lieutenant in a Tyrolean sharpshooters' regiment. He was wounded and taken prisoner on the Russian front. When Russia collapsed, he joined the Ukrainian army. After the war he settled in Horodenka to practise law and was active in the Ukrainian Radical Party. As a prisoner of war he had contracted typhus and almost died in the epidemic that swept the prisoner-of-war camps.

Later he became gravely ill again and was told that he would die. At the hospital he was attended to by nuns. Their deep religious faith made a profound impression on him, like my first morning in Yablonytsia, when I woke and looked out the window to see the sun streaming in and the houses scattered over the green mountains and then went to church and smelled incense for the first time in my life. My uncle told me that he attributed his salvation to the nuns' prayers. He became a believer, gave up his law practice and went to the seminary in Stanyslaviv. He could have gone to the seminary in the Lviv eparchy, where students were allowed to marry before they were ordained as priests, but he chose Stanyslaviv and became celibate. He was much older than his fellow seminarians, and they called him "Grandad."

Few priests were also qualified lawyers, and when my uncle had been graduated from the seminary the bishop offered him the position of chancellor of the eparchy, but my uncle declined it and said that he wanted a poor parish. And because his health was poor and mountain air was thought to have a curative effect on consumption, he asked for a parish in the Carpathians. This was his first and only parish. When the Soviets came the second time and the Catholic church was liquidated, he went to a village five or six kilometres from his birthplace. He died at a relatively young age of cancer.

By the time I arrived in Yablonytsia, no one regarded himself as a *Rusyn,* or Ruthenian, and Ukrainian identity was completely established. Yet Ukrainian life was weaker here than in the other provinces of Western Ukraine because this was a border area. Poland wasn't completely dictatorial, and it was not illegal to speak about Ukrainian history, for example, although you could not give a lecture on the OUN or openly recruit members for it. But the Polish government did have the power to limit access to border areas, and it used it to throw out organizers and activists. Consequently, the Ukrainian organizations in the villages along the border were small and weak.

Few Poles lived in Yablonytsia. There was one Pole in the village who spoke Ukrainian and was married to a local Ukrainian woman and thus was not typical of Polish bureaucrats. Otherwise the two groups had no social relations, and I never associated with

Poles. The only exception occurred when the Communists came to Western Ukraine. Whenever I managed to get through to my uncle's parish, which was very difficult because of the travel restrictions imposed by the Soviets, I would visit the Polish forester, who lived three kilometres away. Two or three times a week he, his wife and I would have supper and then play bridge.

Four or five Jewish families lived in my uncle's village, and all of them were engaged in commerce or the trades. The furrier, the carpenter and the shopkeepers were Jewish. Under Polish rule, tobacco and salt were state monopolies, and a license was needed to sell them. The Jews were the only ones who had licenses. That was not resented, but what was resented, what struck me as very strange, was that although they were living in a Ukrainian village where there was no Polish presence and although they knew Ukrainian well because they had to conduct business, they spoke Polish and not Ukrainian among themselves. Now I understand that people identify with the strong and mighty rather than with the disadvantaged. There's no percentage in allying with the underdog. Unfortunately it has to be said here that when the Soviets occupied western Ukraine some Ukrainian nationalists were betrayed by Jews, among whom there were pro-Soviet elements. That gave rise to bad blood in later years.

CHAPTER 4

SCHOOL IN THE OLD COUNTRY

After a year of tutoring by Nusia Rovenchuk, my brother was sent to a public school in Yablonytsia, and I went to a *gymnasium* in the provincial capital of Stanyslaviv. There were two or three Polish *gymnasiums*, a German one and a Ukrainian one in the town. These were all government *gymnasiums*. There were also two private *gymnasiums* for girls, one run by the Ukrainian Pedagogical Association and the other by the Basilian nuns. The Poles never recognized us as Ukrainians, and the official name of my school was "Government Gymnasium with Rusyn Language of Instruction." Despite the name, Polish literature, geography and history – it was the history of Poland and not of Ukraine, of course – were taught in Polish. Physical education was also taught in Polish, I suppose because it had a nebulous relation with military service.

Except for a Jew named Nathan Koch, all my classmates were Ukrainians. The "director," or principal, was Levytsky, a Ukrainian who had gone to school with my uncle. The teachers were Polish, Ukrainian and Jewish. Both the principal and the "professors," as the teachers were called, were appointed by the government, and the Ukrainians among them were very cautious about expressing their national sentiments. There were many unemployed teachers, and once a teacher had a position he would toe the line for fear of losing his job. Of the three Polish teachers, one taught Polish language and literature, one history and one physical education. We particularly disliked the latter because he was a *perekynchyk*, or turncoat, a Ukrainian who had Polonized his name and tried to pass as a Pole. He spoke to us only in Polish, and we taunted him by replying in Ukrainian.

On Polish national holidays we were obliged to attend commemorative meetings. The students would assemble in the gym; the choir would sing a song or two, and someone would read a lecture. When Boleslaw Pieracki, the Polish minister of the interior, was assassinated by a Ukrainian nationalist in May 1934, we had to buy black arm bands and wear them on our sleeves for a month and to hold a commemorative meeting. We all felt so insulted by this requirement that our nationalism was only strengthened.

The educational system had just been reformed. Previously there had been four years of public school and eight years of *gymnasium*. Now, public school was six years and *gymnasium* four, and then came two years of *lycée*. The old system was modelled on the Austro-Hungarian system, the new one on the French system. The Poles were great francophiles. At the *lycée* we had a bit of choice and could begin to specialize. There were three types of *lycées*, one for the humanities, one for the classics, where Greek and Latin were taught, and one for the sciences. Not every *gymnasium* had all three. The Ukrainian *gymnasium* chose to have the humanities *lycée*, and anyone who wanted to study the classics or the sciences had to go elsewhere.

The students could live privately, paying for room and board, or they could stay at the *bursa*, or residence. There were two residences, the clerical *bursa*, which had been set up by the bishop and where most of the students were the sons or relatives of priests, and the peasant *bursa*, where the lower classes lived. I enrolled at the clerical *bursa*, which was named after Saint Nicholas. It was run by a Father Konovalets, who also taught the religion classes at the *gymnasium*.

The residence was not elaborate or luxurious. The first thing I did when I arrived was to get my palliasse and fill it with straw. It served as my mattress until the end of the year. By then the straw was so packed that it provided very little cushioning. The beds were placed so close together that we had to walk sideways to reach them. Bedding was not provided, and we had to supply our own, as well as towels, soap, shoe polish, toothbrush and tooth-powder.

We got up when the bell clanged at half past six or seven o'clock and went to wash. There were no showers or bathtubs, just a series of basins. We filled them with cold water and washed our faces and hands. If we felt like it, we would strip to the waist and wash the upper parts of our bodies. In winter few people wanted to do that, and hygiene was not very good. Once a month or so, we were marched down to a steam-bath. By going *en masse*, on a day when there were few customers, we got a reduced student rate. After washing we went to the chapel for mass. Then came breakfast, which consisted of coffee and black bread with rendered fat. Then we'd march to school. Classes started at nine o'clock. The school was just one street over, on Lypova – "Linden" – Street. Like every town in Western Ukraine, Stanyslaviv had a large Polish and Jewish population, and Ukrainians were in the minority. The Ukrainian Catholic seminary, the bishop's palace and the two Ukrainian *gymnasiums* were all on Lypova Street. If one street in Stanyslaviv could be called Ukrainian, it was Lypova Street. After Pieracki was assassinated, it was renamed Pieracki Street. We wore government-prescribed uniforms: caps, trousers and jackets with piping. In the *gymnasium* we had blue piping along the seams of our trousers and jacket sleeves, and in the *lycée* we had red piping. On our left sleeves we wore shields with the number of our *gymnasium*.

There were brief recesses between the fifty-five-minute lectures and a longer one at noon. Lunch, which consisted of a sandwich just like the one at breakfast, was provided by the residence. When the day ended at five o'clock, we went back to the residence for supper. We had meat no more than once a week. The rest of the time we ate buckwheat porridge or cream of wheat. In the spring we'd have radishes with salt and bread with rendered fat. We were always hungry. In the peasant *bursa* the students were given plates or bowls with their portions. The clerical *bursa* wanted to be fancier, and we helped ourselves from large serving platters. Everybody watched to make sure that you didn't take more than your share. Sometimes, if you were slow in eating your soup, you'd come to the main course and find there was nothing left for you. To this day I gulp my food because I learned at the *bursa* that you have to eat fast if you want to get your share.

We came back to the *bursa* directly from school and couldn't go anywhere without permission. The two cinemas in Stanyslaviv showed mostly Hollywood films. Two or three times a year we were given tickets at reduced prices and were marched in to see a picture. I remember we were permitted to see *King Kong* and a musical based on Johann Strauss called *The Great Waltz*. And sometimes we would sneak out of the *bursa* and steal into the theatre.

On weekdays we went to mass in the chapel. On Sundays we marched to mass at the school gym. Once in a while we would assemble at the *gymnasium* and go to a service at the Ukrainian cathedral. I rather enjoyed that because even though we had to march there and back in pairs, we had a chance to go outside and walk along the streets.

At first I was homesick and miserable. I missed my mother, my brother and my uncle. The students were all strangers to me, and some of them were as much as seven or eight years older than I was. It was an army recruit's life. The bedding, the food, the furnishings were awful, verging on the criminal. But human beings adapt to anything, and within six months I had formed friendships and felt at home.

There were no social barriers among the students, and none of them put on airs, but the teachers made it obvious that they preferred some students to others because they were the sons of doctors, lawyers or priests. With only a few exceptions, the teachers were completely unprofessional. If they had any pedagogical training, it was very crude, and I don't know how they could have been termed pedagogues. And the teaching system was medieval, based on memorization and regurgitation. There was no discussion between teachers and students. The teachers told us what we had to know and did not tolerate questions.

The school used the tutorial system, and the better students were given financial assistance if they tutored. We were split up into groups of five or six students, each with its own tutor. Every evening our tutor would look over our notes, explain whatever we didn't understand and help us with our homework. The gap between the students and the teachers was too great for any personal relationships. But the tutors, although they were older and were addressed formally, were nevertheless students, and we related to them better, especially if we had the same tutor for more than a year. Most of the tutors were patriotic Ukrainians, and in our tutorial groups we discussed things that were never mentioned in class, Ukrainian history and politics, for example. Thus the tutors instilled patriotism in their charges, not so much deliberately as by a process of osmosis.

At the school I was a celebrity, a Ukrainian from America, and even the teachers treated me with deference. My classmates never said Canada. North America, in their minds, was a single country, and they always called me an American. Of course, they were very curious about life there. Every boy in Europe read Karl May, a German writer who wrote dozens of books about cowboys and Indians. His books were translated into Polish, and I read them all. My classmates considered me an expert because I had come from America. I had never seen an Indian – there were no reservations in Hillcrest – but I was not going to reveal my ignorance. "Oh yes," I would say, "there were Indians around there." Then I would talk about fighting and scalping, much to the delight of my classmates, who would listen with open-eyed awe.

Once or twice a year the parents' and teachers' associations would organize a dance. They would hire an orchestra, and the boys in the older grades would press their trousers and shine their shoes. The dances were formal, and there was no mingling or holding of hands. The girls sat on one side of the floor and the boys on the other. I would walk over to a girl, bow and ask her to dance, then escort her to her seat, bow again, thank her for the dance and go back to my place. The teachers and the parents would sit and watch like hawks to make sure that we held the girls at a distance when we danced with them. After the dance we weren't allowed to take the girls home, and they would go off by themselves. We were sexually frustrated, and perhaps our urges found expression in our intense political activities.

There was a Ukrainian concert hall that belonged to Sokol, an organization dedicated to physical fitness and sport, but with a noticeable political flavour. It staged meets, sporting events, contests and matches and put on plays and concerts. We were not allowed to take part in such events unless they were organized or sanctioned by the school, which required that they have no political content, but some of the students found a way to sneak away, and sometimes Father Konovalets would give the tutors permission – on the sly, of course – to attend an event.

We had no contact with the Polish and Jewish students, simply because there was no forum in which to meet, but we did have contact with the Germans. We felt a kinship with them because we were oppressed by the same people. I was the one who initiated the contact. We arranged for the German students to invite the Ukrainian students to their prom. I got up at the prom and gave a little speech in German, part of which I remember to this day. "We have often had the opportunity to make one another's acquaintance," I said, "but have never got together." Word got back to my school, and I was called a troublemaker and would have been expelled if it weren't for a classmate who cautioned me to be very careful and never to go near the Germans.

When the Nazis came in, Otto Zinger, who had been the president of the student body at the German *gymnasium*, became chief of the Gestapo for the entire region. I still have his picture in my album, inscribed with the words, "To my friend, in memory of the time of the muses." I was told that because he had grown up among Ukrainians, he was sympathetic to them and helped many of them escape when they were arrested. He probably didn't know that I was a Canadian, and when I saw him in the street in Stanyslaviv in 1940, he said to me, "We're going to have a German repatriation committee here. Why don't you get repatriated to Germany as a *Volksdeutsche*?"

Once in a while my father would send me a letter and enclose a dollar with it. In Poland, a dollar was worth five zlotys, and you could buy a three-course meal or go to a brothel for one zloty. So a dollar was a lot of money.

When my father arrived from Canada, the custodian at the *gymnasium*, who also acted as a messenger for the principal, came to my classroom and called me to the principal's office. I walked in to the room to find my father sitting there. I was amazed because although I knew he was coming, I didn't know when he would see me. My father was impressed: I was wearing a Ukrainian embroidered shirt, and I spoke much better Ukrainian than I had in Hillcrest. "Your father's come all the way from Canada," the principal said to me and then made a magnanimous gesture. "Take the rest of the day off."

Off I went with my father. He soon asked about the teachers, some of whom left a lot to be desired. My math teacher, for example, was so terrible that to this day I don't know any mathematics. He was an old bachelor, and we thought he was queer because he had been unmarried so long. He couldn't explain anything, and if he gave us a question that we couldn't answer, he would swat us. I told my father that the teacher was stupid. My father started lecturing me. How could I call a professor stupid? A lot had happened to me in the three years since I had left Canada. At twelve I had still been a baby. Now I was almost an adult, and I thought the teacher was stupid.

A little later my father suggested that we go eat. At the restaurant the waitress asked whether we wanted something to drink. My father ordered two steins of beer. That was a sign that he was treating me as an equal. In his eyes, I could now have a beer with him. So I forgot about his jumping on me for calling the teacher an idiot and was tremendously taken by the compliment he had paid me by buying me a beer.

CHAPTER 5

REVOLUTIONARY FEVER

My involvement in Ukrainian nationalism came gradually. All the influences that I have mentioned – my uncle, my governess and the environment in which I lived during my first year in Western Ukraine – converged to produce a certain effect. Then there were the political people, writers and priests who visited my uncle. People could not afford to go abroad on holidays, and since the Carpathians were so beautiful they would all visit my uncle. He would put them up and feed them, and if he didn't have a bed for them, there was always the hayloft. Other priests, some of whom he didn't even know, would expect to stay for a week or so without paying simply because my uncle was also a priest and therefore owed them something. His professors at the seminary had the same expectation. Freeloaders would come from Lviv. Osyp Nazaruk, a famous writer, used to come down to our place. Later his widow would often visit my uncle. So would the writers who were staying at her villa. They would hike over, stay a day or two and then hike back. They would all sit down with us for five meals a day: breakfast, second breakfast, lunch, tea and then supper. So there was ample opportunity to discuss current affairs in Warsaw, Lviv and Kiev. I didn't participate in the talk – I would have been slapped down if I had tried – but I listened to everything.

The OUN had a youth section called *Iunatstvo*. You couldn't join the section because you didn't know where to join. Even if you wanted to join and suspected that so-and-so was a member, you couldn't say, "Are you a member? Can you get me in?" You had to be recruited.

As we began to discuss things and voice opinions older students would keep their eyes on boys who showed interest in politics. I was thought to be promising and was watched by the older students for a time. Finally, in my second or third year at the *gymnasium*, Bohdan Mustytsky, who was one year ahead of me, took me aside, questioned me about my opinions and then asked if I wanted to join the *Iunatstvo*. I was happy and proud to be asked to join. I was worthy of belonging to an organization that everyone regarded as an elite, a praetorian guard.

The first test in the ritual of induction was to deliver a package of illegal papers to a person who would identify himself by a code word. I was given the exact itinerary to the place where that person would meet me. I was excited and a bit fearful of being caught with underground literature. When I reached the place by a circuitous route, I discovered that the person waiting for me was my boss. And it wasn't underground literature that I was carrying, but a packet of newspapers. I was being tested to see whether I would obey orders to the letter. There were other tests and then an initiation at which I was given the Decalogue, or Ten Commandments of the Ukrainian Nationalist, and told to memorize it. The Decalogue was illegal, and if you were caught with it you were thrown out of school and sent to jail.

We were indoctrinated by reading underground publications – *Surma*, or "The Trumpet," for example – and then discussing them with our leader to show that we had understood them. At this stage it was all indoctrination and political education. The small-arms training came later. We were organized in three-man cells. Eventually I became a cell leader and recruited two new members. Then I knew the two members under me and the one over me. No one ever knew more members than that. If the chain was broken, at the most three links would be lost.

Eventually new members were allowed to do the real thing – to act as couriers or lookouts, to distribute literature and to tear down a flag. Bishop Khomyshyn of the Stanyslaviv eparchy was roundly condemned by everyone as a *khrun*, or collaborator. Public display of the Ukrainian flag was not allowed. But Khomyshyn got permission to display it along with the Polish flag on 11 November, Polish independence day, to show that the Ukrainians were helping the Poles to celebrate their freedom. We thought the bishop was a traitor. How could he sully our flag by hanging it out with the Polish flag when the Poles beat us and when our holiday was on 1 November, the day we liberated Ukraine and captured Lviv? We therefore took down the Ukrainian flag, so that it would not be dishonoured by being flown with the Polish flag on Polish independence day.

In the summer, when I was staying in Yablonytsia, Khomyshyn would drive over from Stanyslaviv in his Mercedes to freeload off my poor uncle. Not content with the cook we had, he would bring his own cook with him, an old woman who was as imperious as he was. She would present a list of groceries that had to be bought for His Excellency – fresh raspberries or strawberries out of season. I intensely disliked the bishop. In about 1937 he decided to revive the spiritual life of the community by having a mission and bringing in priests to deliver fire-and-brimstone sermons. When he arrived, we had to accommodate him and all his hangers-on. We had a veranda along the length of the rear of the house. The bishop had a room at the end of the veranda. The nuns would sit on the veranda, and when the bishop came out of his room they would fall on their knees and – I never saw anything like this before or after – slide the length of the veranda on their knees to kiss the ring on his finger. To this day the way those nuns slithered along the veranda as if their legs had been cut off and they were walking on stumps strikes me as pagan self-abasement.

I had a very interesting summer holiday in 1937 before I went to the Polish *gymnasium* in Sniatyn. I joined Dmytro Maievsky, a prominent member of the Ukrainian underground, in carrying out an inspection of the terrain, as it was called, in Sniatyn county, going from village to village and contacting people. Our trip was an inspection. We were like inspector generals who would come in to review the situation and evaluate the state of the organization. There were several cells in every village, and we talked to the leader of every one. This was my first higher assignment from the OUN.

The OUN did not have a military structure, and military terms were not used. It was modeled on an administrative organization, with local, regional and provincial executives. The national executive was like a shadow government in which each member had an assigned task. One person was in charge of propaganda and publishing and was responsible for finding newsprint and distributing leaflets. A second was in charge of organization. A third was in charge of military training and operations. A fourth was in charge of finances.

Women had their own cells, probably because the schools were not co-educational. The sexes were kept apart, and a student who walked down the street with a girl would hear about that. I know that there were highly placed women in the organization, Mykola Lebed's wife, for example, who was one of the accused at the Warsaw trial of the OUN leadership in 1934.

The Polish police did not particularly harass me, although there were searches at the *bursa*. The Poles knew that I was a British subject and were cautious in dealing with me. I had come to Western Ukraine on my mother's Canadian passport, and when that expired I got a British passport of my own since there was a British consulate in Lviv but not a Canadian one. I didn't conceal the fact of my passport. I had to carry it with me and to get extensions of my Polish visa.

Of course, there was opposition, although that may be too harsh a term, to the nationalists. In the Pokuttia region there weren't many supporters of the Ukrainian National Democratic Union (UNDO), but the Radical Party still had its adherents. Generally speaking, people disapproved of the OUN because they preferred to be uninvolved and didn't want to make waves. Although the OUN had an anti-clerical strain in it, clergymen were no different from laymen in the support they gave the organization: some were sympathetic; others were opposed to the OUN and the actions that it took from time to time. I remember an action taken by the Ukrainian Catholic hierarchy to impede the headlong rush of young people to the OUN. A big rally was organized in Lviv, and young people from all over Western Ukraine assembled to pledge allegiance to Christ. The slogan was, "Ukrainian Youth for Christ."

The Polish "pacification" of Western Ukraine in 1930 was still vivid in the minds of the people around me.[8] The great famine that occurred in Eastern Ukraine in 1932 and 1933 made less of an impression on us.[9] We heard rumours about it; the Western Ukrainian press published articles about it, and some people even managed to escape from the Soviet Union and to bring out their accounts. But the famine was happening in another country. Of course, that was Ukraine, too, but it was in the USSR, and whether you were next door to the USSR or across the Atlantic from it didn't matter because it was a controlled society and little information got out.

I saw no contradiction between being a Canadian-born Ukrainian and a member of the OUN. It was taken for granted that we would stay in Western Ukraine. That was why my father had sold his property in Canada and come over two years after us. By Western Ukrainian standards my father was rich and could have afforded to buy an estate. I even accompanied him once or twice on long trips to look at land that was for sale. In the meantime he looked after his brother's parish forests and lands and dug a well, fixed up the barns and brought in cattle and horses.

I never talked about politics with anyone except my uncle. He and my father learned that I was a member of the OUN only in 1938, I think it was, when I was involved in distributing leaflets. Levytsky, the principal, had a pretty good idea that I was a member, perhaps through an informer. He called me in after the German incident and asked me in a fatherly way whether I realized the risk I was taking by engaging in such activity. I could be

---

8. In 1930 the Polish authorities in Western Ukraine carried out a particularly brutal series of measures to subdue the Ukrainian nationalist movement. This "pacification" was widely protested in Poland and abroad and did not serve to destroy the nationalist underground.

9. Between 1932-1933 a politically engineered famine in Ukraine resulted in several million deaths. See Robert Conquest, *The Harvest of Sorrow: Collectivization and the Terror-Famine* (New York: Oxford University Press, 1986), Roman Serbyn and Bohdan Krawchenko, eds., *Famine in Ukraine 1932-1933* (Edmonton: Canadian Institute of Ukrainian Studies, 1986) and Marco Carynnyk, Lubomyr Y. Luciuk and Bohdan S. Kordan eds., *The Foreign Office and the Famine: British Documents on Ukraine and the Great Famine of 1932-1933* (Kingston: Limestone Press, 1988).

thrown out of the *gymnasium* and then would have to study privately to pass the *matura*.

The *matura* was the final exam before graduation. Students who had very good marks could be absolved from it. If a student was thrown out of *gymnasium*, however, he had to sit for the provincial exams. All the students in the province got together on the appointed day and were examined by a commission set up by the ministry of education in all the subjects they had ever taken in *gymnasium*, from biology, chemistry and physics to Greek, Latin and German. Most of the examiners were Poles, and the Ukrainians among them were so afraid for their positions that they were no help. Nestor Ripetsky, a writer who passed away in Toronto a few years ago, was the editor of our student newspaper, *Svit pered namy,* or "The World Before Us." I was his assistant. A member of the OUN, Ripetsky published an extract from an OUN publication in the student paper. Someone spotted it, and Ripetsky was thrown out of the *gymnasium* and had to take the provincial exams. He passed, only with great difficulty.

In 1939 Carpatho-Ukraine proclaimed its independence.[10] That was a tremendously important event. It is impossible now to describe the exhilaration, rejoicing and high expectations that were raised. Tiny Carpatho-Ukraine would become independent and serving, in the phrase that harked back to Italy in Garibaldi's time, as a kind of Ukrainian Piedmont would lead the other parts of Ukraine to political independence.

I advanced within the organization simply because I had access to the border of Carpatho-Ukraine through my uncle. Even in ordinary times, the Polish police could order people to leave a *cordon sanitaire* that extended thirty or forty kilometres from the border. Because there was suddenly so much traffic into Czechoslovakia and underground activists from Western Ukraine were being sent across the border, the organization needed someone who knew the area and could help people get across.

---

10. Ukrainians in Carpatho-Ukraine, which was then under Czechoslovak rule, proclaimed an independent Carpatho-Ukrainian state on 15 March 1939. It was quickly suppressed by Hungarian troops with the support of the German and Polish governments.

My job was to find guides and assign them their tasks in getting people across. Crossing the border was not particularly difficult for someone who knew the area and was cautious. Central Europeans were very fond of hiking, and in the late spring, summer and early fall it was not unusual to see people walking in the Carpathians. If the Polish authorities happened upon you, you could say that you were merely hiking. The nearest police station, staffed by three or four policemen, was about eighty kilometres away. When the nationalists began moving into Carpatho-Ukraine, the Polish border guards, who were a uniformed paramilitary organization, were reinforced, but even so there weren't many of them and the Carpathians are not an impregnable barrier like the Rocky Mountains. The guards had guns and German shepherds, but if they were in the vicinity you would hear their dogs barking, and you would know whether they were coming or going. The guides I used were not OUN members, but smugglers who had been crossing the border for years. Many things that were cheaper in Czechoslovakia were bought there and smuggled across the border. Shoes, for example, were very expensive in Poland, and we got all our shoes from Czecho-slovakia.

I would be informed by word of mouth or by coded mail that people, whom I knew only by a cover name, were coming, and recognition signals would be arranged. As soon as I or the guides I had engaged had taken the people over the border, they would be handed over to a local Ukrainian. That summer I must have been involved in getting twenty or thirty people across. Other people went to Vorokhta, which was the next parish to the east, and still others went to the west. So at least several thousand nationalists crossed the border into Carpatho-Ukraine that summer.

We had no idea how the question of Carpatho-Ukraine was perceived in the rest of the world. We did not receive any newspapers from outside Western Ukraine, and all we knew was what the Ukrainian press quoted on the subject. News of the assassination of Colonel Yevhen Konovalets in Rotterdam in 1938, which was a major setback for the Ukrainian nationalist movement, did reach us. The members of the organization went into mourning. We all fasted at least one day and donated the money that would have been spent on food to the organization. The Polish press reported the event in neutral terms. In private, Polish bureaucrats might call you names and belittle your language and culture, but the press tried to maintain certain standards of decency.

In the fall of 1938, after finishing the *gymnasium* in Stanyslaviv, I went to the Polish *lyceé* in Sniatyn. My membership in the OUN *Iunatstvo* had caused Levytsky, the principal of the Stanyslaviv *gymnasium*, considerable concern. He had spoken with my uncle several times about my dangerous activities and finally asked him to send me to a Polish school, away from the influence of the OUN.

When I was going home for the Christmas holidays that year and stopped between trains to visit relatives in Kolomyia, I became so ill that I couldn't continue my trip and went to see Dr. Hankivsky. He found that I had pneumonia and a spot on my lungs. He gave me something to bring down my temperature, and then I got on the train and went home. Later Dr. Hankivsky drove out to take me back to Kolomyia. Snow was falling, and the windshield of his car was covered with frost, and even with his nose to the windshield he couldn't see the road. Then he opened his medical bag and coated the window with Vaseline so that it would not freeze. He had come for me because he had an X-ray machine, which was quite unusual in those days, and wanted to take additional X-rays of me. He brought me back, and then another doctor who lived closer to us came to attend me. It was believed that the clear mountain air would cure consumption, and the rest of the winter and all the spring I lay in bed under an eiderdown quilt beside an open window.

I used my enforced rest to read voraciously. Mrs. Vasievych, the local schoolteacher, had a small library at the school and some books of her own. My uncle also had books, and I read all of them, even the theological books from his days at the seminary. I managed to get Nietzsche's *Thus Spake Zarathustra* in Polish and struggled with it for quite a while. When I looked at it years later I found it no more understandable.

My parents, who had decided that they would live out their lives in Western Ukraine, were now thinking about returning to Canada. In 1938, with war on the horizon, the British vice-consul in Lviv wrote to us several times to say that he couldn't guarantee our safety and wanted us to leave. My father said that he had avoided being conscripted during the First World War by being in Canada and wasn't going to stick around and risk being involved in a second world war. My uncle thought that was wise, and my parents and brother decided to go back to Canada.

Then came the problem of me. I had finished the *gymnasium* and had only one year of *lycée* left. What would I do? I was more mature than someone in this country at the age of eighteen or nineteen and was allowed to make up my own mind. I said that I couldn't return without an educational milestone behind me. In Canada, I'd have to go back to high school. But if I stayed in Western Ukraine another year, I could finish the *lycée* and then apply to any university in Europe or Canada. And so I decided that I would gamble on the war not breaking out, finish the *lycée* and then rejoin my family in Canada. Of course, it didn't turn out that way because they left in May or June 1939 and the war started in September.

CHAPTER 6

WAR AND OCCUPATION

I was in the village of Nazirna, visiting the family of a girl-friend, when the war broke out. Many Ukrainians welcomed it. Now, perhaps, a free Ukrainian state would emerge. Everyone who had a radio was glued to his set, listening to Moscow, Berlin or any other station he could catch. The Germans had powerful transmitters, and we could get a number of their stations. We did not feel that the Germans were bringing liberation, but rejoiced that Poland was crumbling. Poles were the enemy: they had conquered Western Ukraine and reneged on their promises to the Council of Ambassadors to grant it certain rights. No one thought about what the Germans might do to us. Whatever happened could not be worse than what the Poles had done. Little did we know that Joachim von Ribbentrop, the German foreign minister, and Viacheslav Molotov, the Soviet commissar of foreign affairs, had signed a treaty of non-aggression, establishing German and Soviet spheres of influence in Eastern Europe and dividing Poland. We didn't suspect anything even when the Soviets crossed the border on 17 September 1939. Their professed objective was to protect the Western Ukrainians and Belorussians. I clearly remember the way the Red Army was hailed on Polish radio on 17 September. Our friends are finally coming to our aid, the radio said. Now we'll show the Germans!

The immediate question after 17 September was who would get to us first. We listened to the radio and tried to plot the army movements on maps. The broadcasts never told us where the troops were, and in the blitzkrieg conditions there was no stationary front. Still we expected that the Germans would arrive first.

A week or so later, someone ran in with a cry that the tanks were coming. Everyone in the village ran into the street, fully expecting to see Germans. Imagine the horror when the column rolled in and we saw red stars. Crewmen stood in each turret, wearing padded helmets, all of them grimy with diesel oil and dirt, looking more like devils than human beings. People stood thunderstruck, motionless and silent. None of the tankmen made any gestures either. They were almost like robots as they stood in their turrets, turning their heads from side to side to watch the people along the road. Nine or ten tanks went by, and we looked at one another, still speechless.

The Polish government had crumbled in the first few days of September 1939, and there was absolutely no rule for quite a while, even after the Soviets came in, until local self-governments sprang up all over Western Ukraine. The Red Army did not interfere with them. Once the military occupation was consolidated, however, a Soviet civil administration was set up. Its first action was to disarm the Ukrainian militias that had been formed in the villages and towns and to arrest the leaders of the provisional governments that had sprung up, even though some of them were Communists. Kolomyia, for example, was one of the few places where a Communist newspaper, *Holos Pokuttia*, or "The Voice of the Pokuttia Region," was being published in 1939. The editor and publisher was a dedicated Ukrainian Communist by the name of Holub. When I went to school in the fall of 1939 with his step-daughter, he had already been arrested and was never heard of again. In fact, the first victims of the Soviet administration were the members of the Communist Party of Western Ukraine,[11] followed not by the Ukrainian nationalists, as one might expect, but by members of the former Polish administration – judges, policemen, jail guards and landlords. Most of the latter were Poles, but some, curiously enough, were Armenians. Some landlords had fled, but most had decided to stay and do the best they could under the circumstances.

Only after this first wave was an attack launched against the nationalists. It continued without let-up. Arresting all the nation-

---

11. For a history of the party, see Janusz Radziejowski, T*he Communist Party of Western Ukraine, 1919-1929* (Edmonton: Canadian Institute of Ukrainian Studies, 1983).

alists was difficult because before the Soviet occupation the OUN had put the stress not on quantity, but on quality. As an elitist organization, it tried to train the best people to provide leadership. Of course, there was a fear that the enemy would infiltrate the organization, but even greater was the fear that genuine members would turn informer after being brainwashed or tortured. Under Polish rule, the average sentence for membership in the OUN had been two or three years. Now the risk was much greater. There were no trials, and you could be simply taken out and shot, even if you were merely an activist and not a member of the OUN. Yet the organization continued its work, and the number of members increased.

The OUN at this time was in a state of preparation, building up its membership, because it hoped that the Soviet occupation was temporary and that there would be a clash between the Germans and the Russians. Ideological training would have been an added risk, but small-arms training was badly needed. It was very primitive, of course. Our unit had a single firing rifle, and I don't think I ever saw a hand grenade.

Towards the end of 1939, the organization embarked on a mass project. The Soviet announced that they would hold elections to a "national congress" that would determine the legal status of Western Ukraine. All students were required to take a "short course" for political agitators at which they were taught how to organize public meetings and exhort those in attendance to do what was required of them by the party. After finishing this course we all took part in the election process, selecting delegates and compiling lists of voters. The OUN seized the opportunity to make a census for itself. We found someone on every team of enumerators who would provide us with carbon copies of the enumeration lists.

The election was a mockery. The candidates – only one in each district, of course – were nominated by the Soviet authorities. In theory, voters could cross out the candidate's name. If more than half the voters crossed out a name, the candidate would presumably not be elected, but that had never happened in the entire history of the Soviet Union.

In my father's village, the husband of the schoolteacher was a delegate. Once, when we were discussing the congress at my uncle's house, he said, "I think I'm going to vote that Western Ukraine not join the Ukrainian SSR, but become a separate Western Ukrainian republic in the Soviet Union." I argued that this was the same old story of parochialism and regionalism as with Petrushevych's Western Ukrainian People's Republic after the First World War.[12] At the congress, the delegates asked no questions and voted unanimously to be united with Soviet Ukraine.

I went to see my uncle several times before school resumed. His status was immediately affected by the occupation. Church and state were separated; churches were heavily taxed (that was one way to close them down); church lands were nationalized, and priests no longer kept the records of births, marriages and deaths. The official designation for priests was changed, and when they were asked about their occupation, they had to say that they were "servants of a religious cult."

The people showed their opposition to the regime by going to mass, and the churches were overflowing. Even I faithfully went to church because that was a way of opposing official policy. And instead of throwing coins into the collection plates, people made very substantial donations to make sure that the levies were paid and the churches stayed open.

When the schools reopened in the fall of 1939, I went to yet another school in the town of Kolomyia and lived in a *bursa*. The times were very difficult because the system was being radically changed and mass arrests and deportations – always at night, of course – were being carried out. The bridges and railway tracks had been bombed. The post office was not operating, and when it started up again, the service was not very efficient. University and *gymnasium* students were herded into student unions, and the

12. On the Ukrainian national independence movement during the First World War see John S. Reshetar, *The Ukrainian Revolution, 1917-1920: A Study in Nationalism* (Princeton: Princeton University Press, 1952) and Taras Hunczak, ed., *The Ukraine, 1917-1921: A Study in Revolution* (Harvard University Press, 1977).

curriculum was revamped. Polish language and history were dropped, and compulsory courses in Russian, Marxism-Leninism and the history of the Communist Party of the Soviet Union were introduced. And the *bursa* could not get enough food to feed the students. There were many days when we had nothing to eat. If it hadn't been for my friends at the *bursa* whose families tilled the soil in the villages around Kolomyia and brought their children cheese, sausage and smoked pork from their farms, we would have all starved.

Wild rumours were going around because the news from Europe was being censored. In the spring of 1940 the Soviet Union served an ultimatum to Romania, demanding the surrender of the provinces of Bukovyna and Bessarabia. The Romanians did not reply, and the Soviets began massing troops on the Romanian border. Kolomyia, which was close to the border, was the focal point for this military action. I remember standing beside the city hall and watching ranks of infantry, artillery and tanks go by hour after hour. I hadn't eaten for three days, and I passed out. When I came to, I found that someone had pulled me into a doorway.

The Soviet authorities did not know that I was a British subject and a Canadian citizen. It had been to my advantage not to conceal this fact with the Poles. With the Soviets the opposite was true. I was a belligerent: the Soviet Union was allied with Germany, which had declared war on Great Britain.

My first brush with the authorities occurred in the fall of 1939, when I was ordered to go to Sniatyn to get in touch with the regional leader of the OUN, a chap by the name of Hutsaliuk. The difficulty lay in entering the border zone: Sniatyn was on the border with Romania. Gaining access to the zone under the Poles had been difficult enough. Now the difficulties were tenfold. The Soviets immediately established two zones. One was the border zone, about five to ten kilometres wide, which not even functionaries and party members could enter without written authorization from the security organs. After the border zone came a thirty-kilometre sub-border zone. Both my uncle's village and Sniatyn were in such zones. If you wanted to travel in the Soviet Union, you had to have a warrant authorizing you to go to a certain place. When you went to buy a ticket, you showed your warrant and then received service. There were always more applicants for space on the trains than seats. And so there was a gradation of priorities. Those with higher priorities got seats, and those with less urgent matters had to wait for weeks and sometimes months to get on.

I got a travel warrant from a person who was sympathetic to the OUN to travel to a hospital in Sniatyn on the basis that no bed was available in Kolomyia. I knew that it would be difficult to come right into Sniatyn. So I went first to a town within the sub-border region, then walked to Karliv and from there went to Sniatyn, where I met Hutsaliuk.

Ten or fifteen minutes after we parted I was arrested and taken to the local militia. Fortunately, it was the militia and not the NKVD. They had obviously been keeping Hutsaliuk under observation, and shortly after that he was arrested and never heard from again. The militia questioned me about my business with Hutsaliuk. I replied, truthfully enough, that I had known him before the war. We had bumped into each other in the street and had exchanged a few words about mutual acquaintances. The militia didn't quite buy that and kept asking me whay I was doing there.

At this point I produced my travel warrant. Paper was extremely scarce, and pre-war Polish publications were cut up and used on the blank side. The warrant that I had was printed on the reverse side of a topographical map. One militiaman, who was not a local, but had been sent in from the east, pounced on me as soon as he spotted the map and accused me of being a saboteur. He couldn't believe his good fortune in finding a person with a map in his possession. I said that it was the other side that counted. My warrant had been written on the reverse side of a piece of a map only because of the paper shortage. That didn't cut any ice with him. The map was the all-important consideration. He left me for a while – to consult with his superiors, I suppose – and only later was I released and told to go to the hospital. Of course, I immediately left Sniatyn and went back to Kolomyia. That first brush with the law showed the paranoia that even a piece of a pre-war map could produce in these people.

A much more serious brush with the law occurred in early January 1940. The war damage had been repaired to the extent that some trains were running, and I was able to spend the Christmas holidays with my uncle. I went in a roundabout way. The direct route would have been to go from Kolomyia to Deliatyn and then to change to a train for Vorokhta, but the bridges had not been rebuilt, and I had to go from Kolomyia to Stanyslaviv and from there to the Carpathians.

I had a cheap papier-mâché suitcase in which I had packed all my clothes because I wanted to have them washed at my uncle's. As I was getting off the train in Stanyslaviv, the handle broke off. I had to wait several hours at the station for my train to arrive, and I decided to check the suitcase, with my British passport inside it, at the baggage room and to keep only my briefcase with me.

As I was walking about the station, two plainclothesmen approached me and told me to follow them. They took me to Bilinsky Street, where the NKVD had taken over a pre-war Polish jail. The jail was in the centre of the courtyard and was screened from the street by administrative buildings. I was put into a solitary cell. When the Polish regime collapsed, the prison guards fled and the prisoners escaped, leaving havoc and destruction in their wake. When I arrived there, the damage had still not been repaired. The glass in the window was gone, and the cell was unheated. There was only a straw palliasse on the cot. In an effort to keep warm I wore all the clothes I had with me and crouched in a foetal position, but I still shook with cold.

Like everything connected with the police, the interrogations always took place at night. I can understand why the Soviet security forces preferred to work after dark. Fewer people would observe them when they converged on a house to make an arrest. And the likelihood of capturing the person they wanted was greater when that person was probably sleeping in his bed. Still another reason might have been that a person's resistance is lowest at night. He cannot think or react as easily as in the daytime. But the main reason, I suppose, was psychological – instilling terror in the populace. When night fell, people would shake with fear, wondering when the knock on the door would come.

Whatever the reasons, I was always interrogated at night. The guards would come in, order me to put my hands behind my back and march me out of the cell. A sentry with a three-sided Russian bayonet on his rifle would escort me through the prison block, across the courtyard, where I'd get a full blast of the winter cold, and lead me into the administrative building, where the interrogators had their offices. The glass in the windows of the corridors that looked out on the street had been replaced, but the windows in the corridors that looked out on the courtyard still had no panes, and the corridors were as cold as the cells. Outside the interrogator's office the sentry would order me to sit on a bench. Of course, he was adequately clothed. Then an orderly would summon me into the room.

The nicest thing was the warmth. Each room had its own tiled stove and was well supplied with fuel. The temperature was kept in the high seventies, and the interrogators worked in their shirt-sleeves. The chair in which I was ordered to sit was placed right beside the stove, and it was a blessing to come into the warm room after shivering with cold. But when the chill had left my bones I would become warm, then hot, and then start to perspire because my scarf was wrapped around my neck, my collar was pulled up around my ears and I had been marched in with my hands behind my back and not allowed to move. I discovered that during my first interrogation when I began to unbutton my coat, and the interrogator curtly told me not to move.

The temperature changes were obviously deliberate. But most of the pressure was psychological, and the only other incident that approached this kind of physical abuse occurred when the interrogator lost his temper, whipped out his revolver, pressed the muzzle against my forehead and said that he would shoot me like a dog if I didn't come clean.

The questioning followed a peculiar system. I would watch with fascination as the interrogator picked up an ordinary pen, dipped the nib into an inkwell and wrote "*Vopros*," or "Question," on the paper he had before him. He would laboriously write out what he was about to ask, dipping his pen and writing in long hand, then sit back and pose the question he had written out. When I had given an answer, he would write it down and then summarize what I had said. He would not use a stenographer, shorthand or any kind of recording device. I thought that the system was antiquated and out of date, and yet it was the only one they used: question, answer, question, answer.

The questioning centred on the suspicion that I was a counter-revolutionary, a bourgeois nationalist. Sometimes I wouldn't leave the cell for several nights. At other times I would be called out two or three times in one night. This went on for several weeks, and I was becoming concerned. I realized from the questions the interrogator was asking that he had no hard evidence against me, but this did not give me much solace. I knew that many people had been arrested, and I had never heard of anyone being arrested and then set free. I had also heard stories that the Soviets did not respect foreign citizenship and arrested and deported people who were not Soviet citizens. And a mere suspicion of counter-revolution was enough for the NKVD to deport or shoot a person. Who would call them on the carpet for doing so? They'd probably be praised for their vigilance. Having nothing to do but to mull things over, I wondered whether I should reveal that I was a British subject. Although the press was filled with harangues against the spies and saboteurs who had been sent by the capitalist and fascist countries to undermine the Soviet Union, I decided in the end that I would gain nothing by pretending to be an ordinary Soviet citizen. Perhaps my interrogator might even be induced to treat me better.

The next time I was brought in for interrogation, I announced that I was a British subject. The interrogator, who had probably never seen a foreigner, was stunned. He looked me as if I were insane and then cried out for the sentry, who was standing in the hall, to take me back to my cell.

At the next session, he asked the obvious question: could I prove that I was a British subject? I had thought about whether to reveal where my passport was. It was my only proof of citizenship. What would happen to me if they withheld it from me? There were a hundred and one considerations. Under such circumstances people grow up very fast. I was only eighteen years old, but my life was at stake and I could not afford to make a mistake. I said that I could prove that I was a British subject. My passport was in my suitcase at the station baggage room.

When I was brought into the interrogator's office again, the passport was lying on his desk. But, as I had feared, the questioning continued. I had confessed that I was a British subject and therefore was a spy. Who had sent me, and what was my mission? On and on the interrogation went.

Alone with my thoughts in the cell, I considered and reconsidered everything that was said at the interrogations. The interrogator kept asking me whom I reported to. I always said that I did not report to anyone because I was not a spy. Now I decided to change my tactic. When the interrogator asked the same question, I said, "Oh yes, it's not a contact in the way you mean, but I am in touch with the British embassy." The interrogator jumped up with joy. He had finally broken me and I was going to confess. "Ah yes," he exclaimed. "And what have you reported to them?" I replied that I had reported my name and passport number. I had decided that this was a way of cancelling any idea they might have of withholding my passport, of convincing the NKVD that I was under the protection of the British embassy. In fact, I was not. I had written several letters to the embassy and had not received a reply. Then I continued with the truth. Look at the passport, I said. It was issued in Lviv and contained a Polish visa. I had legally come to Poland. The Soviets had come here and liberated the area. What did they want from me?

The police in any country can be paranoid, but the NKVD officers were particularly so, and logic and reason had little effect on them. Yet apparently they bought my explanation, or at least had doubts, and thought that the British embassy knew about me and that there might be embarrassing repercussions if I was deported or done away with. In any event, the day finally came when I was called in to find that all my belongings, suitcase included, were in the room and the interrogator presented me with a piece of paper to sign. It was a solemn undertaking not to reveal anything about my arrest, detention and interrogation. As soon as I had signed the paper the interrogator handed me my passport and said that I was free to go.

Lyceés and *gymnasiums* opened in the fall of 1939, after the Soviet occupation, but universities did not reopen until 1940. When I completed the *lycée* I enrolled in veterinary medicine at Lviv University in 1940. My reason for going there rather than to the medical faculty was that the latter was controlled by Jewish students, who dominated the student union and the Communist Youth League. Many of the Jews were Communist sympathizers, although some of them only pretended to be sympathizers, as did some Ukrainians, simply in order to survive. The faculty of veterinary medicine, however, was controlled by Ukrainian nationalists. The president of the student union was Ievhen Panchyshyn, a third- or fourth-year student. The head of the Komsomol, or Communist Youth League, was Klymkiv, also a Western Ukrainian and a nationalist. The rector, or dean, of the school was Ivan Chynchenko, an Eastern Ukrainian who had been sent in to take control.

On coming to the West, people from Eastern Ukraine sometimes become intoxicated with freedom and go off in all directions. This happened to Chynchenko. He stayed behind when the Soviets were withdrawing in 1941 and then was ordained as a Ukrainian Catholic priest. After the war he came to Canada and became an Orthodox priest. When he arrived in Lviv he was dressed in a shapeless Soviet suit and a cap with the visor turned up, while we still had our Polish clothes, which were of better quality and more fashionable. We couldn't get over the sight of a dean who didn't have a handkerchief and blew his nose in his fingers. Under Austro-Hungary and Poland exaggerated politeness and subservience had been in vogue, and we still followed the custom of doffing our hats, bowing and even clicking our heels to such people as university deans, and we expected that they would respond by doffing their hats, although of course not as high as we did. Chynchenko did not doff his hat and even used the Russian greeting "*Zdravstvuite.*" But his manners and appearance changed very quickly. Within a month he began wearing a hat and doffing it to acknowledge greetings.

The committee that sat on admissions to the university consisted of four people: the chairman of the Communist Youth

League, the chairman of the student union, the dean, and the *pompolit,* or commissar for political affairs. The system of political commissars, which was later abandoned, existed in every Soviet institution, including the universities. Every dean had a political commissar who was the eyes and ears of the party in making sure that there was no subversion or counter-revolution. Of the four members of the admissions committee, three were nationalists and one was a Russian Communist. Being new to Western Ukraine, the Communist did not know much about the situation there and did not have any views about it. The other three members naturally favoured people who were nationalists and could not gain admission to any other faculty by reason of their social origin. I couldn't tell the committee that my father was a miner because there were no mines in the area, and so I said that he worked in a quarry. I had to pass entry exams in three subjects – physics, chemistry and the history of the Communist Party. I passed all three with a grade of excellent.

Then I had to submit my documents. Anyone who applied for a job or admission to a school had to submit an "autobiography," or curriculum vitae, a certificate of social origin and an internal passport. The autobiography I wrote myself, and so that was no problem. But I had no certificate of social origin or passport. These documents were issued by the local Soviet, or council, with the appropriate stamps. Since the days of Austro-Hungary, all of Eastern Europe had been obsessed with stamps. When I started practicing law and former Ukrainian displaced persons came in to certify their documents or to swear out an affidavit, I would have them sign their names. "But where's the stamp?" they would ask. "We don't put stamps on documents in this country," I would explain. They wouldn't believe me. What was a document without a stamp? I was taking their money and not putting on a stamp.

On Panchyshyn's advice, I dreamt up excellent proletarian origins for myself and wrote a statement to the effect that my father was employed in a quarry and did not own any land or other possessions. Then I signed the name of the chairman of the local Soviet. Next to the signature I wrote in brackets, "No stamp." Panchyshyn and I had realized that a rubber stamp could not be made locally. It would be necessary to go at least to Stanyslaviv. And even there they might not have the rubber to make it. So it was not unusual to claim that there was no stamp yet. In the same way I forged a statement from the local Soviet that passports had not yet been issued in the region. Although this was the fall of 1940, the inefficient Soviet bureaucracy had not got around to issuing passports in many places, and the explanation that I came from a remote area where the benefits of the Soviet system had not penetrated yet was accepted.

Panchyshyn and Klymkiv knew very well who I was, and I only had to make sure that when the committee met, everything would look in order, and the local people could say to the commissar, "Yes, we know this place. It's in the mountains. There are no roads or railways yet." The commissar accepted all the documents, and I was admitted to the university. Afterwards Panchyshyn removed the certificate of social origin and the statement that I did not have a passport from my file in case any irregularity came to light.

The next question was where to live. In 1906, the Ukrainian community had built the *Akademichnyi Dim,* or Academic House, on Zelena Street in Lviv, to serve as a university residence. It was nationalized by the Soviet government and was now known as "Residence No. 1." The Academic House had a marvelous tradition, and many nationalist plots were hatched there. The student who assassinated Andrzej Potocki, the viceroy of Galicia, in 1908 had lived at the Academic House. I almost felt as if I were entering a shrine when I walked into the building. A friend who had been my classmate in Stanyslaviv was living there, and we obtained a room with other fellows.

Then came the problem of a passport, one that concerned every citizen. When you arrived at a place, you had to present your passport to the local militia. When you left, you went back to the militia to report where you were going. To keep the peasants from deserting the collective farms, they were not issued passports. They didn't need passports to get on a train, but they couldn't register with the militia when they arrived at their destination and were likely to be arrested.

This requirement caused me considerable difficulty. The

authorities knew that I was registered as a student at the university and appeared on the roll at Residence No. 1. Without a passport I could not register with the militia, and I could not bluff my way and say that no passports had been issued in my village. The university authorities might not know, but the militia would make it its business to find out whether passports had been issued in Yablonytsia. So instead of bluffing, I did not register. A month or six weeks went by, and the militia realized that I had not registered and came looking for me. They were not the NKVD and didn't come in a Black Maria in the middle of the night, but they did look for me during working hours in the lecture halls, the library and my room. Friends would tell me that the militia had been asking people whether they knew where I was. I realized that I was bound to lose this race.

One day the militia came to the residence for me. I started to explain that I had meant to register and would do so now. The funny thing was that they didn't arrest me or demand that I register immediately. As soon as they left, I figured that the game was up, withdrew from the university and went to stay with a friend who was enrolled in medicine.

After several weeks the militia found me again. "Get out of Lviv and don't ever show up again," they said to me. "If you do, we'll lock you up and throw the key away." I was happy to get off with a tongue-lashing and went back to my uncle's. Again I was caught, taken to the railway station, put on a train and told to get out of the border zone. I realized then that I might be thrown in jail, deported to Siberia or shot. My situation was hopeless: without a passport I couldn't go to school, get a job or earn any money and had to live as a gypsy, going from village to village and not staying anywhere more than twenty-four hours.

My next hope was to get a living permit so that I could legally stay in one spot. The militia had told me that the regional NKVD in Yaremche could give me one. I went to the regional NKVD office and found the people there to be more businesslike and less abusive than the militia. They listened to my story with sympathy and then, for fear of being held to account if I proved to be a traitor, said that I had to go to the provincial NKVD people. I went to them, and they, too, told me that I was at the wrong place. This was a matter for the regional NKVD. But I was there and they told me to come here, I said. "The idiots don't know what they're talking about! Go back there." I went back to the regional NKVD. "No, no, this is their job, go back to the provincial NKVD," the regional NKVD said.

I tried appealing to their sense of logic and reality. "Look, I'm here," I said to them. "You can't wish me away. I was here when you 'liberated,' as you put it, Western Ukraine. I had a legal Polish visa. Now I'm asking you for a Soviet visa. Permit me either to reside here or to leave." This was the first time I had brought up the idea of being permitted to leave. Since I was a spy, they answered, they could neither allow me to reside anywhere nor let me leave. "What am I supposed to do?" I asked. "Rise in a hot-air balloon to live between heaven and earth? I'm here. Why can't you accept that and do whatever is necessary to formalize the actual state of affairs?"

No appeal to reason or emotion had any effect. Getting that piece of paper that would allow me to live in one place was impossible. Things were desperate. Finally I went back to the NKVD and said, "You're not giving me a residence permit. Obviously I have to live somewhere. The only relative I have here is my uncle. Let me go live in his village."

"Go ahead and stay with your uncle," they said.

"Give me something in writing so that the border police won't pick me up, as they have in the past, and kick me out."

"No, they won't. Tell them we said you could stay there."

I had already written to the British embassy and not received a reply. When I was at the embassy later, I learned that none of my letters had been received. Now I borrowed money from my uncle and sent a telegram to the embassy. I said that I had a British passport and needed assistance in leaving the country. Perhaps because the NKVD was not monitoring the telegraph or because someone slipped up, my wire went through. The embassy replied with a letter, asking me to submit my passport. How stupid these people in their ivory tower are, I thought. How naive to think that I would entrust my passport to the mail. So I sent a letter in which

I wrote, as diplomatically as I could, that I did not want to risk sending the only proof of citizenship that I had. The embassy replied that my telegram had given the number of my passport, that all passports, no matter where issued, were registered at the Foreign Office and that there would be no problem in issuing a duplicate. With that assurance, I sent my passport. In due course it was returned with a Japanese transit visa stamped in it. The accompanying letter said that the embassy could not help me get a Soviet exit visa. I would have to go to the provincial NKVD office in Stanyslaviv, where I had been several times in an effort to get a residence permit. I had to make several trips because something further was always required, and although I was promised each time that I would receive an exit visa, the NKVD did not seem to be in a hurry to put it in black on white. But eventually I was called in to pick up the visa and asked exactly when I would leave.

CHAPTER 7

DEPARTURE

I went back to my uncle's village to pack. I had a ticket for a "special fast train," which had been put on for the express purpose of taking out foreigners, but it took twelve days to travel from Moscow to Vladivostok. I couldn't risk not taking food because I'd starve in that time. What food should I take? My uncle was of help because as an officer in the Austro-Hungarian army during the First World War he had been wounded in battle and had been held as a prisoner-of-war in Siberia. He told me that because they were great tea-drinkers, Russians carried their own tea, sugar and utensils when they travelled, and it was possible to get boiling water and to brew tea at every station. Since bread would grow mouldy, my uncle's housekeeper dried loaves of bread in the oven, then washed a pillow case and filled it with the dried bread, as well as with several heads of garlic. My uncle firmly believed in the medicinal value of garlic and maintained that it was good for the heart and the blood and prevented arterial sclerosis. Finally I packed a piece of salt pork.

I couldn't leave on the appointed day in March 1941 because the weather was bad. All my clothes were still wet after having been washed and couldn't be packed in a suitcase for that long a journey because they would become mouldy.

Some time after midnight, after I had already gone to bed, the NKVD came to the door. They asked for my papers, and when I presented them, they held on to my passport. This is it, I thought to myself. They had lulled me into believing that they would let me go and now they had come to take me away to prison or exile in Siberia. I asked whether I was under arrest. No, they said, but I would have to go with them to their office. I smoked then. So did my uncle, who always managed through his connections to get cigarettes, even when they were in short supply. He placed in my hands a package of a hundred cigarettes called *Chervonyi prapor,* or "Red Banner," and some money. The parting was heart-rending because I did not know where I was going and what the future had in store.

As it turned out, we took the train to the county seat in Yaremche. There I was taken to the NKVD office, which I had visited so many times when I was trying to get a residence permit. The NKVD officers were quite civil and told me what places I ought to see in Kiev and Moscow. We sat there for six or seven hours, until the next train was due, and then got on and went to Stanyslaviv. I wondered why we had got off in Yaremche. There was no rhyme or reason to it, but that's how things were done.

In Stanyslaviv I was taken to the provincial NKVD office. There I discovered that the NKVD wanted to make sure that I would not act against Soviet interests. The officer questioned me about my attitude towards the Soviet Union and how I would assess my experiences after having resided there. Naturally, I was not going to say that the system was lousy and that I had hated every minute of it and so tried to sound as positive as I could without being hypocritical. Finally the NKVD man openly expressed his concern that I might speak ill of the Soviet system when I got back to Canada. Looking at me with steely eyes and speaking very unemotionally, he pulled out a list of names and read them to me. My uncle and all my aunts were on the list. "These are your relatives," the officer said. "They're remaining, and I'm sure that you would not want to endanger them in any way."

This brings to mind a bit of post-war history. When my mother and I arrived in Western Ukraine, we visited my father's second cousin Mykola Ostafiichuk. He had inherited quite a lot of land from my great-uncle and, having saved money in Canada, had bought more land and was very well off. His house in Karliv was one of the biggest. My grandfather's house was small, and the family was large, and during summer holidays, when my father's stepsisters came home from teaching school, we would always stay with Ostafiichuk. He was extremely hospitable and helpful, and his house was our home away from home. After the Soviet

Christmas carollers with a *vertep*, or Nativity scene, in Hillcrest, Alberta, 1911.

The Hillcrest branch of the Ukrainian Social Democratic Party in 1915.
Stanley's father, George Frolick, is third from the left in the bottom row.

Workmen Time for the

	1.	2	3	4	5	6	7	8	9.	10	11	12	13	14	15	16	17	18
1. January.																		
2. February.																		1.
3. Mark.																		
4. aprill.																		
5. may.																1.	1.	1.
6. June.	1.	1.	1.	1.		Bubyje ajtualiny.						1.	1.	1.	1.	1.	1.
7. July.		1.		1.	1.	1.	1.	1.		1.	1.	1.	1.	1.	1.	1.	
8. august.		1.	1.	1.	1.		1.		1.	1.	1.	1.	1.	1.		1.	1.
9. September	1.	1.	1.		1.	1.	1.	1.	1.	1.		1.	1.	1.	1.	1.	1.
10. october.	1.	1.		1.	1.	1.	1.	1.		1.	1.	1.	1.	1.		1.	
11. november.	1.	1.	1.	1.	1.	1.		1.	1.	1.	1.	1.		1.	1.	1.	1.
12. December	1.	1.	1.	1.		1.	1.	1.	1.		1.	1.	1.	1.		

Сім місяців і пів робил

Month of January to December. 1910.

21	22	23	24	25	26	27	28	29	30	31.	Total Days	per Day	AMONT	
												1.50		
		1.	1.	1.	1.	1.	1.		1.	1.	13.		19..	50.
1.	1.	1.	1.	1.		1.	1.	1.	1.		19.		28.	50.
1.	1.	1.			1.	1.	1.	1.	1.	1.	25.		36.	50.
1.		1.	1.	1.	1.	1.		1.	1.	1.	26.		38.	
1.	1.	1.	1.	1.		1.	1.	1.	1.		24.		35.	
1.	1.	1.		1.	1.	1.	1.	1.	1.		25.		36.	50.
	1.	1.	1.	1.	1.			1.	1.		24.		35.	
1.	1.	1.	Приѣсавъ доеваіѵе ..								16.		24.	
											172		$. 253	00.

іѵї на Морісей. В.С.

910. рк

George Frolick in 1917.

The Hillcrest co-op in May 1918. George Frolick is third from the left in the second row.

George and Mary Frolick in their car, October 1919.

George and Mary Frolick in 1920.

(Opposite) Stanley Frolick's birth certificate.

Government of the Province of Alberta

BUREAU OF VITAL STATISTICS
DEPARTMENT OF PUBLIC HEALTH

Certificate of Birth

This is to Certify, that the particulars of the undernoted Birth, which is on record in this Department, are as follows:

Name of Child   WASYL PROLAK

Date of Birth   SEVENTH 7 day of JULY 19 20   Sex MALE

Place of Birth   HILLCREST, ALBERTA   Name of Father YURKO PROLAK

Birthplace of Father   KARLOW, AUSTRIA   Occupation of Father LABOURER

Name of Mother before Marriage   MARIA MACIFORUK   Birthplace of Mother KULAZO, AUSTRIA

Registered at HILLCREST, Alta. on the TWENTY-NINTH day of SEPTEMBER 1923

Registrar   FRANK SMITH

Given under my hand and seal of the Department of Public Health at Edmonton

this TWENTY-SECOND day of JANUARY 1926

Donald MacKie

Deputy Registrar General.

№ 13721

Stanley Frolick and his parents.

The hospital at Le Havre where Stanley Frolick spent a month in 1932.

Stanley Frolick (holding the whip) with his mother, brother and their relatives in Western Ukraine.

Stanley Frolick's uncle Vasyl in the 1930s.

Stanley Frolick's passport.

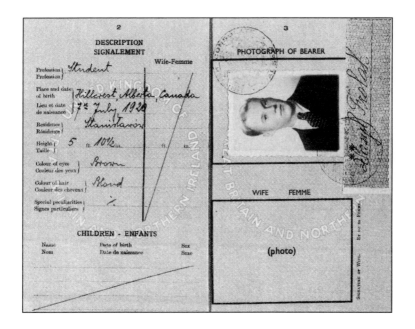

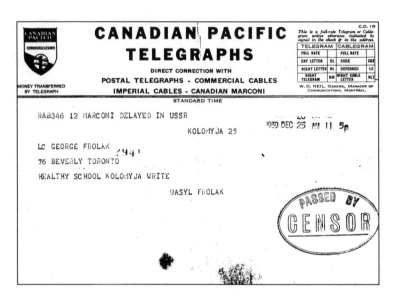

Telegram from Stanley Frolick to his father, 25 December 1939.

Opposite: Stanley Frolick's report card,
Kolomyia, 15 June 1940.

УРСР

Народний Комісаріат Освіти

АТЕСТАТ

ВИДАНО ЦЕЙ АТЕСТАТ *Фролякові Святославові Юрійовичу*,

(прізвище, ім'я та по батькові)

ЩО НАРОДИВ*ся* В 19*20* РОЦІ, В ТОМУ, ЩО *він*

(від, нова)

НАВЧАВ*ся* В *Коломийській* СЕРЕДНІЙ ШКОЛІ №*1*

міста Коломиї

(села, міста)

Станиславської області

(району, області)

ЗАКІНЧИ*в* ПОВНИЙ КУРС ШІЄЇ ШКОЛИ І ВИЯВИ*в*
ПРИ *відмінній* ПОВЕДІНЦІ ТАКІ ЗНАННЯ:

З української мови	*посередньо*	З географії	
З української літератури	*добре*	З фізики	*добре*
З російської мови	*посередньо*	З хімії	*посередньо*
З російської літератури	*посередньо*	З геології і мінералогії	
З арифметики		З астрономії	
З алгебри	*посередньо*	З іноземної мови (*німецької*)	*посередньо*
З геометрії	*посередньо*	З малювання	
З тригонометрії	*посередньо*	З креслення	*добре*
З природознавства		З співів	
З історії		З фізкультури	*відмінно*
З Конституції СРСР і УРСР	*добре*	З військової справи	

№ *2*

25 червня 1940 р.

М. П.

ДИРЕКТОР ШКОЛИ *Шимайло*

УЧИТЕЛІ: Б. *Лащук*

Stanley Frolick (fourth from the left in the bottom row) at a UNYF convention in Toronto, 1941.

The Eastern Canadian executive of the UNYF en route to the first UCC congress, Winnipeg, 1943. *From left to right:* Vasyl Hultai, Ivan Vasylenko, Stephanie Sawchuk, Stanley Frolick, Volodymyr Hirniak.

Opposite: UNF delegates to the first UCC congress, Winnipeg, June 1943.

JESSOP STUDIO

GROUP OF DELEGATES OF UKRAINIAN NATIONAL FEDERATION PARTICIPATING IN
ALL-CANADA UKRAINIAN CANADIAN CONGRESS - WINNIPEG MAN. JUNE 22-24 1943
HELD BY UKRAINIAN CANADIAN COMMITTEE

Joint session of the Ukrainian Canadian Committee and Ukrainian Congress Committee of America, Ottawa, March 1945. *First row, from left to right:* Dr. Longyn Cehelsky, Dr. Wasyl Kushnir, Stephen Shumeyko, Rev. Josaphat Zhan. *Second row:* Stanley Frolick, Dmytro Halychyn, Anthony Hlynka, Dr. Luke Myshuha, Wladimir Kossar.

Stanley Frolick shortly before going overseas in 1945.

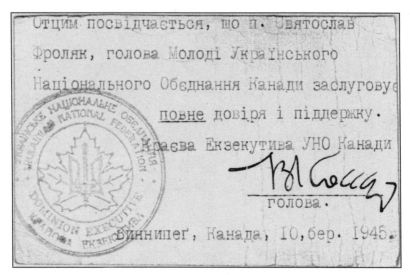

Отцим посвідчається, що п. Святослав
Фроляк, голова Молоді Українського
Національного Обєднання Канади заслуговує
повне довіря і підтримку.
Краєва Екзекутива УНО Канади

голова.

Винніпег, Канада, 10,бер. 1945.

A card signed by Wladimir Kossar, head of the Ukrainian National Fredration, confirming that Stanley Frolick, head of the UNYF, deserves "*complete* trust and support."

The Ukrainian Canadian Servicemen's Association building, 218 Sussex Gardens, Paddington, London.

UCSA members at a sing-song, November 1945. *Third from left:* Stanley
Frolick.

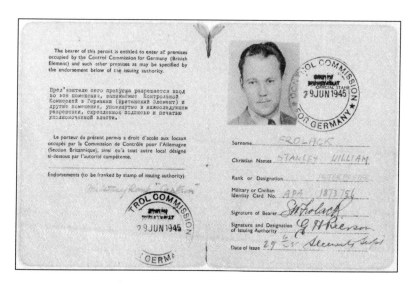

Stanley Frolick's permit from the Control Commission for Germany.

**UKRAINIAN
CHIEF LIBERATION COUNCIL**
SECRETARY-GENERAL OF FOREIGN AFFAIRS

Headquarters, December 2, 1945.

TO WHOM IT MAY CONCERN

    This is to certify that Capt. S.W. Prolaok is a
plenipotentiary representative of the Secretariate-
General for Foreign Affairs of the Supreme Ukrainian
Liberation Council and is also authorized to act on
behalf of the Ukrainian Insurgent Army (U. P. A.)

(M. Lebed) Sec.-Gen. for For. Aff.
SUPREME UKRAINIAN LIBERATION COUNCIL

Stanley Frolick's authorization to represent the UHVR and UPA.

CURB representatives visiting the Ukrainian DP camp in Heidenau, Germany, 19 December 1945. Stanley Frolick is the second of the three men in uniform.

Members of the UCSA and CURB in London, 1945. *From left to right:* G.R.B. Panchuk, Peter Smylski, Joseph Romanow, George Kluchevsky, Stanley Frolick.

Joe Romanow and Reverend Wasyl Kushnir in London, 1945.

Dymtro Andrievsky, Danylo Skoropadsky, and G.R.B. Panchuk, London, 1945.

PUT **TRINITY** ON
the side of
GOOD GOVERNMENT

ELECT
STAN FROLICK
PROGRESSIVE CONSERVATIVE

MONDAY, JUNE 18ᵀᴴ

For Election Information
COMMITTEE ROOMS

935 Bloor St. W.   LE. 4-6393
704 Queen St. W.   EM. 4-6171

A leaflet from Stanley
Frolick's campaign.

Stanley and Gloria Frolick in the 1950s.

occupation I would also come and stay with him, even though his house was in the sub-border region and I was there illegally. After the war, my father went to Ukraine twice. The first time he was not allowed to visit his village, and his family came to see him in Chernivtsi. Suspecting that my father might be questioned about me, I told him that if any Soviet official asked about me he should say that he didn't know me. My father gave me a strange look, as if he thought that I was an egomaniac, but didn't say anything. When he got back from his trip, however, the first thing he said to me was, "How did you know that they were going to ask about you?"

When his plane landed in Kiev, two civilians were waiting at the bottom of the steps for him.

"Are you Yurii Froliak from Canada?" they asked.

"Yes."

"Do you know Sviatoslav Froliak?"

My father remembered that I had warned him about this. "No," he said. "There are lots of Froliaks in Canada, and I don't know all of them."

The second time my father went to Ukraine – I think it was in 1979, three years before his death – he found a person who promised to get him permission to see his village. In return he wanted a number of articles from Canada. My father bought these articles and went to Lviv. The chap arrived from Kiev, collected his articles, and my father received his permission to visit his village for one week. He stayed with Ostafiichuk, and all the people in the village came to see him and threw one party after another.

While my father was visiting his village, Ostafiichuk and his second wife told him a story. Between 1946 and 1952 Ostafiichuk was constantly harassed by the NKVD. He would be picked up, taken to the NKVD headquarters in Sniatyn and questioned about my whereabouts. Ostafiichuk explained that I had left Ukraine, but the NKVD was convinced that I was underground. I suppose that the Soviets evacuated Western Ukraine in June 1941 so hurriedly that they either destroyed or lost their records. By that time many people, among them close friends of mine, had been arrested, and

some of them may have named me as a member of the underground.

Then an even more curious thing happened. Karliv was the only
village where there were Froliaks, but it had very many of them.
At one time they had all been related, but now the relations were
so distant that they didn't count. A fellow who had the name
Froliak invited my father to his home. My father didn't know him,
but the man pleaded so earnestly that my father finally agreed.
When he arrived at his house, the man explained that he wanted
my father to go back and tell me how he had suffered in my place.
He had the same name and surname – Vasyl Froliak – as I did. He
was born the same year I was, and his father was named Yurii just
like my father. He had been arrested and had spent three years in
Soviet jails, he told my father. He didn't know how he survived
the first two years because he was beaten incessantly. From the
way he was questioned he knew that they were after me. He kept
saying that they had the wrong man, but they wouldn't believe
him.

"Your name is Vasyl Froliak?"

"Yes."

"Born in 1920?"

"Yes."

Then they would hit him again and say, "Confess. You're a
counter-revolutionary!"

After two years they stopped beating him – perhaps they had
concluded that he was telling the truth – and then finally released
him. Vasyl told my father that he bore me no grudge. He simply
thought that I would want to know what I had missed.

The NKVD also beat Ostafiichuk, on one occasion so severely
that he was left unconscious. His wife thought that they were
going to kill him. She threw herself on her husband's supine body
and said to the NKVD officers, "If you want to kill somebody, kill
me, because what good am I if my husband is dead? How am I
going to bring up my children without my husband?" The NKVD
men then went away. She called for help and got her husband into
the house, and he eventually recovered.

After the questioning in Stanyslaviv, m passport wa returned to me and I went back to my uncle's to pick up my luggage. My uncle had sold his sleighs, his riding horse and his good English saddle and in this way obtained more than four thousand roubles. I bade him a tearful farewell because I realized that I would never see him again and so much had been left unsaid, and could not be said, and bought a ticket to Lviv.

When the train stopped at Stanyslaviv, an NKVD officer got on and without either concealing himself or acknowledging me sat down near me and travelled with me to Lviv. Now that I was a foreigner who was legally leaving the Soviet Union and not a tramp who was hounded from village to village by the militia, I had to make use of the facilities provided by Intourist and stay at an ornate Baroque hotel built in Austro-Hungarian times and known before the war as the George Hotel.

In the hotel room I put down my suitcases and decided that my first task was to get a ticket for the rest of my journey. My uncle had suggested that I pay a call on Metropolitan Sheptytsky. Once I had my ticket, I would visit a few friends and see the metropolitan. As soon as I opened the door and stepped into the hall, the door to the next room opened and my NKVD guardian angel appeared. When I walked out of the hotel, he followed me. I realized that the NKVD wanted me to know that I was being followed and decided not see any friends so as not to endanger them.

The Intourist people in the hotel directed me to the railway station to get my ticket. When I asked for a ticket to Moscow at the station, I was laughed at. "You can't just come and get a ticket," I was told. I said that I knew that, but here was my passport and my exit visa. That was fine, but then I was told that there was such a demand for tickets that people had to wait for days and sometimes weeks to get one. Without a written travel order, getting a ticket was a hopeless task. It took me several days to get a ticket. It was for Kiev, not Moscow, but I figured that at least I was advancing along the way.

As I was getting off the train in Kiev, I saw a man walking up and down and calling out my name. "Sprechen Sie Deutsch?" he said when I answered. I said that I did. He apologized for not speaking English. The only foreign language he knew was German. I suppose he assumed that because I was a foreigner I did not speak Ukrainian or Russian. I figured that I would play along with him, and from then on we spoke German. He told me that he was a representative of the Intourist office in Kiev and took me by street-car to the Intourist hotel.

As the Intourist guide and I walked out of the station to board a streetcar, an old beggar said, in Russian, "Give me a coin, *gospodin.*" I was shocked: he spoke in Russian, he was a beggar, and he addressed me as *gospodin*, or "sir," a term that had not been used in the Soviet Union since the revolution. It was a terrible first impression.

The Intourist hotel – it was known as the Continental – had been built before the First World War and had a history of its own. During the period of Ukrainian independence, it had been the headquarters of the *Sichovi Striltsi,* or Sich Sharpshooters, who were commanded by Yevhen Konovalets and Andrii Melnyk. It was there that they made their plans to overthrow the Skoropadsky regime and establish the Directorate.

Kiev was a disappointment for me. For one thing, the weather was terrible all four or five days that I stayed there. It had been snowing, and the streets were covered with slush mixed with horse manure. The sky was leaden, wet snow was falling, and the air was damp and chilly. The city itself was run down. No work had been done since the First World War in refurbishing the buildings, and the paint was faded. I had idealized Kiev, the city of a thousand golden domes, that stood on the hills above the Dnieper River. I suppose that in the summer, when the sun was shining and the trees were green, the city was beautiful, but in March 1941 it was terrible.

There were certain sites that I would have loved to see – the seat of government during the period of independence or the library where the historian Mykhailo Hrushevsky worked – but I was so terrorized by the thought that I was being followed that I did not ask any questions. I merely walked around the streets, without asking directions. Even when I saw a church, I would think that it looked familiar but could not be sure what it was.

The Intourist people said that they would get a ticket to Moscow for me and I would not have to stand in line, but getting a ticket was not much easier than it had been in Lviv. The Supreme Soviet had been called into session, and the deputies were descending on Moscow from every corner of the Soviet empire so that they could obediently raise their hands and unanimously adopt each and every proposal put forth to them. They liked to travel in style – that was one of the perks of being a deputy – and I had to spend four or five days in Kiev before I could get a ticket.

My first impression of Moscow was one of strangeness. This was a city unlike any I had seen. It had, for me, a flavour of the East, of Genghis Khan and Tatar hordes. The Intourist hotel that I was assigned to was the Savoy on Rozhdestvenskaia Street, just off Red Square. It had been built in the nineteenth century and was past its prime, but there were still signs of opulence – a huge chandelier in the lobby, a magnificent staircase and heavy velvet drapes. The ceilings were high and the furniture was from the nineteenth century, but the mechanical things did not function well. The elevator periodically broke down; the toilets did not flush; the hot water – and sometimes the cold – did not run.

I don't know whether I was followed in the streets, but I was certainly kept under surveillance at the hotel. The telephone would ring in the middle of the night, and when I picked it up nobody would answer. I don't understand why the authorities thought it necessary to go this extreme because there was a *dezhurnaia*, or floor lady, on every floor, located strategically so that you could not enter or leave any room on that floor without being observed by her.

Unlike Intourist in Kiev, which had not extended any "hospitality," the Moscow Intourist people recommended that I go to museums, the Bolshoi Opera, for which they could get tickets, and, of course, the Lenin mausoleum in Red Square. I went to the mausoleum out of curiosity. There were huge queues outside, but foreign tourists went to the head. The Soviet citizens in the queue did not complain because they realized that the people placing the tourists there were associated with the NKVD. We were told exactly how to behave: we could not carry any briefcases or parcels; we were not to speak while we were in the mausoleum, and we had to keep moving.

The mausoleum was a huge granite structure with steps leading below ground. There we filed past a coffin containing what purported to be Lenin's remains. The lower portion of the body was concealed by the casket. The face and the chest were under glass. We shuffled past the casket, looking at it until we were out of range, and then went up the steps into Red Square.

I found it hard to believe that I, a Ukrainian born in Canada, was in Kiev and Moscow. What am I doing here? I often thought. Is this real? In the train to Kiev and then to Moscow I had stopped at stations – Berdychiv, Konotop and other places – that I knew about from Ukrainian history and literature. It was all dream-like. Moscow, of course, was different. I had never been to a city with a square as large as Red Square. The Kremlin walls and Saint Basil's Cathedral were ornate and bizarre and seemed like something out of a fable, intended to delight children. Other buildings, especially the modern ones, were horrendous examples of the Stalin Gothic style of architecture.

At the main department store, or GUM, in Moscow I found that many of the things displayed in the windows were not available. There were queues – for bread, sugar and textiles – all over Moscow, as there were in Kiev, where they were much longer. The people were shoddily dressed. Both men and women wore padded jackets and horrible caps with earflaps, and on their feet they had *valenki,* or pressed felt boots, and rubbers. There was no colour in their clothing.

In Moscow I drew stares because all the men wore long padded pants while I was dressed in plus fours, hand-knitted stockings tied up with woolen strings at the end of which big fabric balls hung down like Christmas ornaments and a pair of sturdy mountain-climbing boots. I had bought them second-hand in the black market in Lviv. The uppers were fine, but the soles were worn, and since there was absolutely no leather to be had, even in the black market, I bought a piece of tire and had a shoemaker put on rubber soles. I also had a suit made for me by a Jewish tailor in my uncle's village from a Polish army officer's uniform. I came to Canada wearing that suit and those boots. Communists whom I encountered in Toronto greeted me with radiant smiles as someone who had just come from the workers' paradise and asked me how "our government" was doing. I would lift my foot and show them the sole of my boot. Their faces would sink, and they would curse me for having been bribed by the fascists to defame the Soviet Union.

Finally I got a ticket on the trans-Siberian express to the Japanese port of Tsugaru, across from Vladivostok on the Sea of Japan. I was in a "soft-class" compartment. Soviet trains had two classes, but, because the Soviet Union was supposedly a classless society, they were called "soft" and "hard." In the soft class, the seats were upholstered and there were four people to a compartment. In the hard class, people sat on wooden benches, and there were no compartments. The Intourist people did not ask me whether I wanted soft or hard class. I suppose it was first come, first served. When I peeled out my remaining roubles and received my ticket, I saw that it was a piece of cardboard with the words "Moscow-Vladivostok" printed on it. Below that were "hard class" and "soft class." The words "soft class" had been crossed out with an indelible pencil.

At the hotel I had met a Polish girl from Lviv who was leaving for the United States. Jadwiga had been born there and had returned to Poland as an infant with her parents. She had no recollections of the United States and spoke no English. Six or seven months pregnant, she was leaving her husband and her parents and going to a strange country. When I was talking to Jadwiga, I saw that her ticket was the same as mine except that the words "hard class" had been crossed out. I didn't say anything to her, but went up to my room, got an indelible pencil and with a little bit of work managed to change my ticket from "hard" to "soft." To survive in the Soviet Union, you have to live by your wits. If you observe the rules, you fall victim to the system.

Jadwiga and I went to the station together and found that we would be sharing a compartment with the chief rabbi of Lithuania and his new bride. I was surprised to see that he was a young man because I had thought that, as in the Christian churches, advancement comes after years of service. The rabbis who were under him would stop by to consult him, and on the Sabbath they would come in to hold a service. In that case I would leave the compartment, although they never asked me, in order to give them more room. Some of the other rabbis were elderly, but they all deferred to the chief rabbi. We communicated in Polish because he was from Vilnius, the old Lithuanian capital, which had been seized by the Poles after the First World War.

In Moscow I had also met a Jew named David who had emigrated to the United States, become an American citizen and then had returned to Poland. He was the only person on the train who spoke English, and we became fast friends. Instead of sitting in the compartment with the pregnant Polish woman, the rabbi and his bride, I spent most of my time in the dining-car with David.

Most of the passengers on the train were Jews. There were three Poles – Jadwiga, another woman and an engineer – and a dozen Norwegians who had fled from occupied Norway to neutral Sweden and were on their way to Canada. The Royal Norwegian Air Force was being trained in Toronto, at barracks in Stanley Park, behind a Loblaws building that now houses a multicultural television station on Lakeshore Boulevard. All the Norwegians who managed to escape from Norway made their way to this "Little Norway," where they got their air force training, and then went overseas to fight the war. I became very friendly with one of them, and we sailed together from Japan to Canada. He lent me some money on the ship. I looked him up in Toronto to give him back his money, and we would see each other from time to time.

The train had at least fifteen carriages and engines at the front and back. Except for the conductor, the trainman and the crew, there was not a single Soviet citizen. All the passengers were either leaving the Soviet Union, as I was, or were in transit. Many of the Jews had managed to leave countries occupied by, or allied with, the Germans. They held Central American passports. Costa Rica, Nicaragua, Colombia and Panama were impoverished, and their consuls in New York supplemented their revenue by selling passports, sometimes for as little as seventy-five or a hundred dollars. American Jews would take pictures of their relatives in

Europe to the consulates in New York and buy passports. Then they would mail the passports to the United States embassy in Moscow, which represented the interests of the Central American republics in the Soviet Union. The embassy would surprise the relative by sending him a letter and saying that it had a passport for him and would be happy to assist him in being repatriated to Panama or Costa Rica.

Soviet officials did everything in their power to give our train priority, and regularly scheduled trains had to pull off onto sidings so that we could go by. Other trains stopped for long periods. Our train stopped only at major stations for ten or fifteen minutes to take on fuel, water or provisions or to change engines. Although I ate the salt pork that my uncle's housekeeper had packed, I had no need for the dried bread or the tea. The dining car was well stocked; the prices were reasonable, and once or twice I even ordered the sweet Soviet champagne.

We were not allowed to get out when the train stopped at a station, but in temperatures of twenty or thirty degrees below zero we had no desire to do so. The only interesting landscapes were in the area of Lake Baikal. Everything else was covered with snow, and between the larger stations there seemed to be no habitations. The windows in the train were covered with thick layers of hoar-frost and ice, and when I breathed on the glass to make a hole I saw only white nothingness. However, I did notice that a soldier with a rifle guarded every bridge and tunnel, no matter how insignificant. How did they get that man there to stand guard, I would wonder. Was he dropped down from the sky? To this day I am mystified.

We finally arrived in Vladivostok, and the train pulled into a siding near the docks. The train crew informed us that a bus would come to take us to the docks, where we would clear Soviet customs and board a Japanese ship to cross the Sea of Japan.

The passengers included old people, children and infants and even sick people. The disembarkation was handled inefficiently. There was one bus, which could take only thirty people at a time, and the procedure went on all day. All this while the lavatories in the train were kept locked, and to ensure that nobody got off the train, armed sentries marched back and forth on both sides of it. People therefore relieved themselves in the corridors and compartments. It was the worst thing I had ever seen or smelled. And we couldn't reason with the train crew and make them understand that it was better to open the lavatories than to have people defecate in the corridors. The Soviet mind is not open to logic. The crew had been told that we were all foreigners and would have to be guarded to make sure that nobody escaped to sabotage some installation.

The second indignity came when we were robbed by the customs officers. I had nothing of value, but the customs officers did find a cross-stitch photo album with a picture of the three friends with whom I had roomed at the Academic House. They had been called up for military service and were stationed with an artillery unit in Odessa. My friends had sent me a picture of themselves in uniform – overcoats and the peaked caps with big red stars known as *budyonovkas* – and on the reverse they had written, *"Dorohomu Slavkovi, druhovi pravdyvoi ideinoi dumky,"* which can be translated roughly as "To Dear Slavko, a friend who shares the true belief."

The customs officers immediately singled out the picture. It was forbidden even to take a picture of a private in the street, and here a foreigner was carrying a picture of three Soviet soldiers. I explained that they were friends with whom I had gone to school. Then the customs officers asked me what kind of belief was meant in the inscription. I assured them that there was only one true faith, communism. I don't know whether the explanation satisfied them, but they did confiscate the picture. I was very worried. How stupid, I thought, to take this picture with me. My friends weren't identified, but the inscription included the date and the place, and the authorities could have tracked them down. Under these suspicious circumstances – a foreigner leaving the country with a picture of them – they would have had great difficulty. Fortunately, when I met one of my three friends after the war, he told me that he had never heard anything about the picture. The Soviet system had been too slow and inefficient to track them down in the few months before the German-Soviet war broke out.

I lost only the picture, but many of my fellow passengers lost valuable possessions. It was arbitrarily laid down, for example, that you could not take out more than one fur. Many of the ladies had astrakhan coats and fur collars. The customs officers would say that that was two furs and rip the mink or fox collar from the coat and confiscate it. The women would protest and say that they were in transit through the Soviet Union and had purchased the furs outside the country. This made no difference. In the category of jewelry, only one ring was allowed. The women often had both engagement rings and wedding bands. The customs officers would examine them and take the most valuable one. We could not protest because we were on the threshold of freedom and could not take a chance until we had crossed it.

When we boarded the ship, we were struck by the horrendous realization that it had no cabins. The hold was one big empty space that ran the length of the ship. The floor, as is the custom in Japanese homes, was covered with straw mats, on which we would have to sleep. There were no linens or blankets, and no curtains or screens for privacy. Only small Japanese pillows stuffed with seaweed and covered with oilcloth were provided. The food was equally primitive: the Soviets had pocketed the money we had paid for our fare and had given the Japanese only enough to transport us. For breakfast we got a cup of tea and a slice of bread. For lunch, a cup of tea, a slice of bread and an orange. For supper, a cup of tea and a slice of bread.

During the second day on the ship, the crew distributed customs declarations for us to fill out. The forms were in Japanese and English, and David and I were the only ones who understood English and could fill out the forms. One of the questions was how much money and valuables we had with us. Many of the passengers were carrying concealed valuables and had to decide whether to keep them in concealment or to declare them. They held a meeting, at which the chief rabbi presided, and after a lengthy discussion they decided to declare the valuables, on the grounds that the Japanese were probably only concerned whether they had enough money for their short stay in the country. This proved to be the right decision. No valuables were confiscated.

David and the chief rabbi asked if I would help fill out the customs forms. I was glad to do so. David and I got a table and two chairs from the captain, set ourselves up at the end of the room and worked day and night to complete all the forms before we landed. Each passenger would come up to us and submit his passport, and I would ask, in Polish or German, whether he had any valuables. It was truly remarkable when in those confined quarters, with no screens, walls or even sheets or blankets to hide behind, the travellers would bring out diamonds, gems, gold coins and paper currency. The ingenuity that went in to finding places of concealment was truly stupendous. Handles of suit-cases and soles and heels of shoes were hollowed out. Being Orthodox Jews and knowing that they would not get kosher food in Soviet restaurants, many of the passengers had brought tins, jars and bags with food. One family was carrying a paper bag containing home-made doughnuts. These ingenious people had steamed open the bottom, inserted two or three American hundred-dollar bills and then glued the paper back. Who would have thought to examine a greasy bag with a few stale doughnuts in it?

Then the ship's captain, who spoke English, announced over the loudspeaker that we would be met by Japanese customs officials in port and would have to hand in our declarations and provide proof of "landing money," fifty dollars I think it was. I had never heard of this requirement and had no money.

When my father left in 1939, he gave me his gold pocket watch. It was on a chain to which an American two-and-a-half-dollar gold coin was attached. At critical moments – when I stood at the city hall watching the troops go by, for example – I had regarded the watch both as a gift from my father and as an insurance policy. If things were really bad, I could always sell the coin. But when I was living at the Ukrainian *bursa*, someone stole the watch one night. Then when we went through Soviet customs in Vladivostok, we were robbed not only of furs and jewelry, but of roubles. I still had some roubles, and when the customs officials asked whether I had any Soviet currency I handed them over. Although I didn't bemoan the loss of the roubles because they were not worth much, I did have a vague idea that I would be able to claim them at a Soviet embassy. But the officials looked at me as if I had gone mad when I asked for a receipt. What right did I have to demand a receipt?

I asked Jadwiga whether she would lend me the landing money. She had only sixty dollars, which was barely enough for herself. Nor did David have enough money. But I discovered, to my surprise, that although he had never been to Japan, he knew what to expect there. He told me, for example, what both the official and the black-market exchange rates between the American dollar and the yen were. He also told me that representatives of a Jewish refugee committee would be meeting us when we landed in Japan. He would speak to them and see what could be done. Not wanting to rely totally on this bit of advice, I asked to see the captain. He was arrogant and imperious, but he did grant me an audience.

"What is this about landing money?" I said. "I have no money, but I am a British subject. Does that make any difference? And what happens if I don't produce the money?"

The captain's reply was the most chilling piece of news I had ever received. The passengers would disembark at Tsugaru, and the ship would return to Vladivostok. Anyone who could not produce the landing money would not be allowed to step on Japanese soil and would be taken back to the Soviet Union. When the ship had finally left Vladivostok for Japan, I had almost fallen to my knees and offered a prayer of thanksgiving for being rid of that terrible country. Now the captain was telling me that my jubilation may have been premature and I could be going back. I would have rather jumped overboard and drowned than gone back. What would I have done in Vladivostok, half way around the world from Yablonytsia and the Carpathian Mountains and with no money?

"What would you suggest I do?" I asked the captain.

"Send a cable to the Canadian legation in Tokyo," he advised me. "I am sure that they will help you if you are their citizen."

"All right," I said. "Will you send a cable?"

"Yes, but it will cost you five dollars."

"I haven't got five dollars," I said. "Will you trust me?"

He would not. Where would I get five dollars? I went back to Jadwiga and explained my situation to her. She gave me the money, and I went back to the captain, who sent a cable to the Canadian legation.

We arrived at Tsugaru during the night, and in the morning I went up to the captain to find out if he had received a reply to my cable. There was no reply, and the Japanese officials were coming. "Is there anything you can do to help?" I asked the captain.

"No," he said, "it's not up to me. They won't permit you to disembark in Japan without money. You can't be a burden."

"I won't be a burden," I said to him. "I'm sure that the Canadian legation will help me."

"No, rules are rules. You've got to have fifty dollars."

When I left the captain's quarters, I bumped into David. "Can you imagine?" I said to him. "They'll be sending me back."

"Let me look around and see if there are people who can help," he said.

I knew that there were people with money – the family with the hundred-dollar bills in the doughnut bag, for example – but I was too proud to beg. In the back of my mind was the hope that at any moment a reply from the Canadian legation would arrive.

Eventually the Japanese officials came on board, accompanied by representatives of the Jewish relief committee. Two or three immigration officers collected the customs declarations, looked for evidence of landing money and stamped the passports with entry permits.

Then David came over to me and said that one of the Jewish representatives, a lawyer from Poland named Dr. Greenberg, wanted to see me.

"I understand that you were very helpful to my people, and I want to thank you," Dr. Greenberg said to me after David had introduced us. "David tells me that you have a bit of a problem."

I explained that I had no landing money. I had borrowed money to send a cable to the Canadian legation, but there had been no reply. Now I would have to go back to Vladivostok.

"Oh no, we can't have that," Dr. Greenberg replied. "Let me see your passport." He looked at my passport and said, "Oh, you're British, not Canadian."

I explained that my passport had been issued in Lviv, where there was a British consulate, but not a Canadian one. Dr. Greenberg was from Lviv. "There's no problem," he said. "Come with me."

He took me to the Japanese officials, and before I knew it they had stamped my passport and told me that I could collect my suitcase and disembark.

I went over to Dr. Greenberg to thank him. "You must have told them something because they're letting me go," I said.

"Oh yes, we posted a bond for you," he replied. "We guaranteed that you would not be a burden to the state. As a matter of fact, do you have any money at all?"

"Not a cent," I said.

"What do you expect to do when you get off the ship?" he asked.

"I don't know," I answered. "I'll probably go around and see if I can borrow money for a railway ticket."

"Well, here," Dr. Greenberg said, and he handed me forty or fifty yen, which was equivalent to about fifteen or twenty dollars. "This is enough for a ticket to Tokyo, one night in a hotel and food."

I was overwhelmed by this unexpected kindness and thanked Dr. Greenberg profusely. Then I asked him for his address so that I could send him the money when I got home.

"This is not a loan," Dr. Greenberg replied. "This is a gift. You've helped us. We've helped you. Now we're even, and you don't owe us anything."

The suspense had ended. I knew for the first time that I was truly free of the Soviet Union. And when I walked down the gangplank onto the dock, I found the wet misty morning almost balmy after the frost and ice of Siberia. In the train to Tokyo, I saw that cherry trees were in blossom. During the two years that I had been in the Soviet Union, I had seen an orange only once, at the tourist hotel in Moscow, and that cost five roubles, or one dollar. Here, the first person I encountered was a Japanese peasant woman in a conical hat and a cape made of palm fronds or grass.

She was selling baskets of fruit containing a pineapple, a few mandarins, oranges and some other fruit. And all this cost the equivalent of ten cents.

I was struck by the Japanese efficiency and cleanliness. The bullet train to Tokyo was fast and punctual. The countryside was immaculate, with every bit of land cultivated and nothing wasted. The people were extremely courteous. Although Japan was at war with China, there were no shortages. Everything was so unbelievable, so quaint and unusual, that I felt as if I had gone from hell to heaven.

In Tokyo, not knowing how to find the Canadian legation, I decided to take a taxi. The taxi driver would follow the streetcar tracks, which were even with the roadway, accelerate, then turn the motor off and coast along the tracks. Then he'd start the engine again, accelerate, shut it off and coast again. I knew the Japanese were extremely practical, but this made no sense to me. Starting up again and again used more gasoline than maintaining a constant speed would, but the practice was quite prevalent because I observed it each time I took a taxi.

At the British embassy in Moscow the staff had been cold and officious. With my Slavic nature, I had embraced my fellow British subjects, but they had treated me like something that the cat had brought in from the street. At the Canadian legation I got a much better reception. The man I dealt with even asked me about my financial situation. I told him that I had a little money.

"Well, we can advance you some money," he said. "How much would you like?"

With the yen I still had from Dr. Greenberg and the hundred or hundred fifty dollars advanced by the legation, I felt pretty good and decided to celebrate my freedom by going to the Imperial Hotel, which had been designed by Frank Lloyd Wright and was renowned for its luxury. I stayed there one night – that was all I could afford – and then went to Yokohama, from where the ship to Canada would be sailing and where I moved into the Bund Hotel.

War-time restrictions had already been imposed in Japan. There was no live entertainment, for example, because the Japanese felt that it was not becoming to make merry while their soldiers were dying in combat. The only entertainment available was in the geisha houses and bars. The geisha houses were not brothels. Sex was available, of course, but for the most part they served the function of English clubs, as places to relax with friends and to be entertained by the geishas, who were better educated than most Japanese women because Japanese society was sexist and women existed only to cook for men, to wash their feet and scratch their backs and to keep their beds warm.

At the Bund Hotel in Yokohama, I met a number of my fellow passengers from the trans-Siberian express. A day or two after I moved into the hotel, the child of one of the women who had been on the train with me became very ill. The woman was crying and said that she needed a doctor. Most of the educated Japanese spoke English, and I found myself pressed into service as an interpreter. I went to the hotel manager, and he called a British doctor who was residing in Yokohama to look at the child.

When the doctor had finished his examination, the woman asked how much she owed him. The doctor told her what his bill was in yen. The woman replied that she didn't have yen, but she did have American dollars. The doctor agreed to take them at the rate of six yen to the dollar, whereas the official rate was four yen. You could buy a meal for one yen, so the difference was substantial. As we were going out, the doctor said to me, "If anyone else has any dollars he wants to exchange, I'll be glad to buy them at the rate of six yen to the dollar." Foreigners could buy American dollars – up to $150, if I remember correctly – with Japanese yen at the official exchange rate at the bank if they presented their passports and showed their exit visas. I took the $150 worth of yen that I had been lent at the Canadian legation to a bank and asked for dollars. With the dollars I went to the doctor and got six yen to the dollar and immediately had fifty per cent more than I had received at the legation. Later I found someone who gave me six and a half yen to the dollar. All the fellow passengers with whom I was staying at the hotel found my interpreting services indispensable and were happy to oblige me when I gave them yen and asked them to buy dollars for me.

What was I to do with all the money? I couldn't take out more than I had declared in my passport without running the risk of being charged with black-marketing. So I bought a few luxuries for my family. Woollens were hard to come by, but there was no shortage of silk, and I had a tailor make pyjamas to measure from pure silk, as well as a magnificent kimono for my mother. I also bought cigarette boxes and spent money on food, the hotel, taxis to Tokyo, which I visited almost every day, and a trip to Kyoto, the old imperial capital. For the first time in my life I was managing to earn money, albeit not by the sweat of my brow, and did not have to count every penny. It was a great life, and I ended up staying in Japan longer than I had thought I would.

Although I had regularly written to my parents, I never received a reply. But that did not mean that they were not getting my letters, and I hoped that one or two might get through, especially since I avoided anything that might give the Soviet postal authorities cause to confiscate the letter. As it turned out, my parents did not receive a single letter. The first message that they had from me was a postcard from Japan. It came as a tremendous surprise. Not having heard from me, they seriously entertained the thought that I had been arrested or killed. It never entered their minds that I was alive, but that my letters were not getting through. They applied to the Canadian Red Cross and the International Red Cross in Geneva. They even wrote to the Soviet embassy in Washington – Canada did not have diplomatic relations with the Soviet Union – and were informed that a search would cost five dollars. My father thought that it was lousy to charge money for a humanitarian cause, but he sent the money and never heard anything until two weeks after I arrived in Toronto, in May 1941, when he received a letter from the embassy saying that I was alive and well in Kolomyia.

When my Japanese transit visa was about to expire, the Canadian legation told me to go to the police in Tokyo to have the visa extended. The reception was barely civil, very unlike the Japanese, who were always bowing and smiling. I attributed this to my British passport. The Japanese had already signed the

Tripartite Pact, which allied them with Germany and Italy, and I was technically an enemy of Japan. The police official looked at my passport and told me to come back. During my second visit he made an anti-Semitic remark. I must have had a puzzled expression on my face because the official said, "Well, you're a Jew."

I said that I was not a Jew.

"But it says right here in your passport that you're a Jew." British passports never referred to racial origin. "Where does it say that?" I asked.

The official pointed to a Japanese stamp. "Your organization, the Jewish committee, put up a bond for you."

I said once again that I was not a Jew.

Now it was the official's turn to be perplexed. "If you're not a Jew, why do you have this stamp in your passport?"

I began to explain the circumstances in which I had acquired the stamp. When I mentioned that I was Ukrainian, the official wanted to know what that was. And I when I said that I had come from the Soviet Union, he asked what I thought of life there. His demeanour changed completely when I told him that it was terrible. "We'll be very glad to extend your visa," he said. "How long do you want it for?"

"Oh, I don't know, a week or two."

The official gave me three weeks and said that I could always come back if that wasn't enough. As I was leaving, he observed that my story was very interesting. Would I mind telling it to some of his friends? Being naive, I readily agreed, and the official fixed a time for the following evening. I wondered why we would meet after office hours, but the official was so friendly that I was not concerned.

The following evening, several men, all with smiles on their faces, asked me to tell them my story. They were particularly interested in the Soviet Union and asked whether there was great dissatisfaction. I said that in Western Ukraine there certainly was. The regime was maintained only by force, and the people were only waiting for a chance to get rid of the Communists. What friendly people these Japanese were, I thought at the time. Only years later did it occur to me that they were intelligence agents and were pumping me for all the information I could give them.

When I was boarding the *Heian-Maru,* the ship that I travelled on from Yokohama to Vancouver, one of my interrogators was there to see me off. He shook my hand, wished me well and even gave me a Japanese artifact as a memento of our meeting. I had been brought up to reciprocate a gift with a gift. When you go to a village in Western Ukraine and bring the people something, they feel that they have to give you something in return. I thanked the official and said that I could not give him anything in return, but then I remembered that I had a brass Hutsul ring with a cross-stitch etching on it. I took out the ring and explained that it was not valuable, but it was folk art, done by Ukrainian mountaineers, and I wanted to give it to him in return. He was rather touched by that ring.

In Vancouver, a Canadian customs official added up the value of the pyjamas, kimono and other gifts that I had bought and calculated the duty. It came to a rather large amount. I had spent a lot of my money crossing the Pacific. The *Heian-Maru* was a luxurious ship, with bars and sumptuous six- or seven-course meals. The meals were paid for, but the bar service was not. To pass the time I played bridge. My foursome included a retired British sea captain who had lived for thirty or forty years in Japan and now was moving to Victoria. He told great stories about life in Japan. When the great fire of Tokyo occurred, the Japanese went berserk and started massacring Koreans to vent their hysteria. While the captain was telling us about these atrocities, we would have a few Scotches. He would buy one round, and then I would have to reciprocate. And so when the customs official in Vancouver questioned me, I broke down and cried.

"Look, I was separated from my parents by the war," I said to the official. "I went through hell, and now I'm so happy to be coming home that I bought a few presents for my parents and brother, and you're asking me to pay customs duties."

"All right, pass on to immigration," the official said.

The immigration officer's questioning was so primitive that

when I was debriefed again by the RCMP in Toronto I said exactly what I thought of him. He no doubt wanted to make sure that I was the person named in the passport. "I see you're from Hillcrest, Alberta. Where is that?" he asked. If I was an impostor, I would have certainly looked up Hillcrest in an atlas. Then the officer asked several other questions that an impostor would have informed himself about – what the capital of Alberta was and what occupation Albertans were engaged in, for example.

After stopping in Vancouver for several days to visit my mother's sister and her husband, I got on a train and went on to Toronto. There, while being debriefed again by the RCMP, I met George McLellum, who was then the chief of counter-intelligence and later became the superintendent of the RCMP. He was one of the few knowledgeable people whom I encountered. He knew a lot about the Communist system, and there was no naivety about him.

My parents had gone from Western Ukraine to Toronto rather than to Hillcrest because my father had sold our property in Alberta and had bought a commercial building in Toronto, with a Dominion store as a tenant on the ground floor and apartments on the top floors. My parents lived in one of the apartments, and my father worked in a steel mill at Bathurst and Dupont Streets.

Their reception of me was joyous and tearful. We sat up night after night, talking about what had happened. I learned that my father had drifted away from Ukrainian organizations. By no stretch of the imagination could he have been called an activist any more. And he had become more tolerant of other points of view. What struck me most was the change in my brother. When he left Western Ukraine, he was still a child. Now he spoke in a deep voice, and I could hardly recognize him.

CHAPTER 8

ON WITH THE STRUGGLE

When I was leaving Western Ukraine, the OUN told me to get in touch with Wladimir Kossar in Canada. I wrote to him as soon as I arrived. Europeans are very sensitive about titles, and it is important to address a person properly. I had been given Kossar's name, but I couldn't call him simply "Mr. Kossar." I recalled having been told that he had commanded a brigade in the Ukrainian army during the First World War. Figuring that the commander of a brigade must have been at least a colonel, I addressed him as "Dear Colonel Kossar." Later I found out that he had been only a captain and his title was *inzhynir*, or "engineer," because he had been graduated from the Ukrainian agricultural school in Podebrady in Czechoslovakia. Perhaps because of my faux pas or because he was suspicious of a person who claimed to have just arrived from the USSR – Yevhen Konovalets had been assassinated in 1938 by a man who claimed to be an envoy from the nationalist underground in Soviet Ukraine – Kossar never replied to my letter. I soon found out that he was the head of the Ukrainian National Federation, or UNF. I went down, looked it over and in short order became a member. Once again I had to work my way up through the ranks. After I had been a member for a few months I got on to the executive and then at the next election was elected president of the local Toronto branch, and so it went. No one asked me about my experience with the OUN in Western Ukraine, and Kossar never mentioned my letter to him. Whatever position I reached with the UNF was earned by my work in its ranks and not by my record with the OUN.

Canadians regarded the UNF with suspicion at this time.[13]

---

13. On Canadian government policy toward ethnic minorities during the
    Second World War see Norman Hillmer, Lobomyr Luciuk and Bohdan

Newspapers were publishing articles and letters to the editor in which it was accused of being pro-nazi. The Hetman movement, which was a viable organization at that time, with its own newspaper and representation in the Ukrainian Canadian Committee, evoked just as much suspicion, simply because the Germans had helped install Hetman Skoropadsky as the head of a monarchist government in Ukraine in 1918. Even in Ukrainian circles, the idea that he was a puppet lasted well into the 1940s.

All the Ukrainian organizations in Canada were nationalistic in the sense that they stood on a platform of an independent and sovereign state. The only country they could look to for help in the realization of their goal was revisionist and anti-Communist Germany, which made no bones about its intention to redraw the map of Europe. These hopes became more pronounced when Hitler attacked the Soviet Union in June 1941. Although no one knew what would follow after he had achieved military victory, it was logical to assume that he would dismember the Soviet empire and create, for his own purposes, a Ukrainian state.

Ukrainians in Canada found themselves in a predicament. Through its link with Britain, Canada was now allied with the Soviet Union, but the anti-Communist and anti-Russian feelings that Ukrainians had nurtured for so many years could not be changed overnight. How could they suddenly open their arms to their mortal enemy? Many people in Canada went overboard, not realizing that we were allied with Stalin only because Hitler had attacked him. A military alliance made by accident and maintained out of expectation of mutual benefit did not mean that we had to accept our ally and his philosophy altogether. Of course, many people did accept that philosophy and became apologists for the Soviet Union. Communism was not so bad, they said, and the West had to revise its attitude. Those who had experienced the evil of communism could not subscribe to this new attitude. The same argument could be made about Germany. You could acknowledge it as an ally and accept its military help without accepting the

---

Kordan, eds., *On Guard For Thee: War, Ethnicity and the Canadian State, 1939-1945* (Ottawa: Committee for the History of the Second World War, 1988).

ideological basis of the Third Reich. Many Ukrainian-Canadian leaders saw Germany as a tool for reaching a goal, but differentiated between that and the acceptance of nazism.

Western Ukraine had been socially stratified, but the political movement in the area had been fairly uniform, at least among young people. The multiplicity of Ukrainian organizations and of points of view that I encountered in Canada in 1941 struck me as detrimental to the community. More threatening than the political division was the animosity that these organizations manifested towards one another. Their suspicions took the form of both ideological and physical confrontations. And that was despite the creation of an all-embracing umbrella organization called the Ukrainian Canadian Committee.[14] The organizations within the UCC were competing against each other in the most aggressive and un-parliamentary fashion. Each watched the others to make sure that they were not trying to exploit the situation for their own benefit and spent more of its energy on outmanoeuvering them than on promoting the common cause.

The common cause was clear to me. As part of a single Ukrainian people, Ukrainians in Canada had to do everything possible to throw off the shackles of foreign domination. Only political independence can allow a nation to live freely and develop its potential. Except for the Communists, all the Ukrainian organizations shared the goal of an independent Ukrainian state. But each group had a different conception of the state and of the methods that would be used to achieve it. Some organizations – the Ukrainian Self-Reliance League, or USRL, for example – in principle had a hazy ideal of Ukrainian sovereignty but in practice were not very devoted to it. The USRL had come into being in order to promote Ukrainian independence, as its Ukrainian name, *Soiuz ukrainskykh samostiinykiv,* indicates. A *samostiinyk* is one who stands for independence, an "independentist." But over the years the USRL had lost sight of its original purpose.

---

14. For more on the origins of the UCC see B. S. Kordan, "Disunity and Duality: Ukrainian Canadians and the Second World War." MA thesis, Carleton University, 1981.

Yet the USRL at least paid lip service to the ideal of independence and promoted the narrower goals of well-being for Ukrainian Canadians, pride in one's origin and retention of language and culture. What I give the USRL particular credit for, because no other organization pursued that goal with such tenacity, was encouraging young people to study at university. For that purpose the USRL organized residences for students from rural areas whose parents could not afford to send them to school. Before the arrival of the post-1945 immigration, the vast majority of the Ukrainian-Canadian intelligentsia supported the USRL. Of course, it was so successful in part because the residences gave it an opportunity to indoctrinate people with its own point of view. The young people who came from rural areas to study at university were mostly Catholics. At the residences many of them were converted to Orthodoxy and became supporters of the USRL.

The Hetmanites also wanted an independent Ukrainian state, but their philosophy would not permit them to consider any form of government other than a monarchy. In my opinion, it was ludicrous to suggest that Ukraine would adopt a monarchical system at a time when monarchies were falling by the wayside in most countries. In addition, there was no basis for a monarchist ideology in Ukraine. The Ukrainian psyche was not suited to monarchy, and there was no monarchist tradition. There were certainly monarchists. Some clergymen in Western Ukraine were monarchists, and Osyp Nazaruk, the editor of *Nova zoria,* or "New Star," proposed a kind of conservative monarchism. The newspaper was closely linked with the Ukrainian Catholic church, especially the eparchy of Stanyslaviv and Bishop Khomyshyn, whom so many people despised. Much of the hostility towards Khomyshyn was transferred to the newspaper. I certainly never met any person of my own age in Western Ukraine who professed to be a monarchist.

The Brotherhood of Ukrainian Catholics, or BUC, on the other hand, was – and in my opinion still is – an amorphous organization with no clearly defined aims. It was simply a lay organization of Catholic parishioners who paid only lip-service to the goal of a free Ukraine.

By the time I arrived in Canada, the physical combats among Ukrainians – the Hetmanites and the UNF, for example – had only recently ceased. On one occasion in Toronto UNF supporters went to a hall where the Hetmanites were celebrating Skoropadsky's coming to power in 1918 and provoked a battle royal that ended with people breaking off chair legs to batter one another over the head. Charges were laid, and the matter went to the Supreme Court. The lawyer who defended the UNF extracted a high fee, but it nonetheless lost the action.

I soon became a much-sought-after public speaker, and meetings were called to hear what I had to say. My first speech took place within a week after I arrived, at the Ukrainian People's Home on Lippincott Street in Toronto. I made no bones about what I had seen and what Soviet rule meant for Ukraine. I always invited questions, and there was often quite a bit of discussion. The Communists were lying low because the Canadian government had banned their organization, the Ukrainian Labor and Farmer Temple Association, or ULFTA, but they came to my lecture and asked questions from the floor. They were immediately hooted down.

In fact, the Communists had been the first Ukrainian Canadians to approach me. My aunt was married to a man who was very active in the ULFTA, and they came to see me at my parents' apartment. Much to their chagrin, they discovered that I was not singing the praises of the Soviet Union. They shook their heads in disbelief at the notion that someone who had lived in the Soviet Union could sell himself to the capitalists and denigrate communism. Word soon spread that I was a threat to the Communists, and from then on they constantly attacked me.

The UCC had little power at that time. In theory, it represented the existing organizations, but most people gave their allegiance to their own organizations. The UCC was an arena in which each organization strove to become more influential in the eyes of the community and the government of Canada. This attitude never permitted the UCC to become an organic outgrowth of the Ukrainian community. The organizations had been born out of need and in that sense were organisms. The UCC, by contrast, was a mechanical contraption without a soul.

The great weakness of the UCC was – and still is – the built-in veto power. Every proposal had to be adopted unanimously, and one dissenting voice was enough to thwart it. The only solution was to hold more meetings and to decide who would censor whom. If Kossar was to speak, it was agreed in advance that his speech would be submitted for approval to the USRL. And a speaker from the USRL would have to obtain the approval of the Hetmanites. People checked one another out as if they were not united by political bonds, but were belligerents.

I was a member of the eastern Canadian executive of the UNF, which included Ontario, Quebec and the Maritimes, although there was no organization in the Maritimes, except perhaps in Sydney, Nova Scotia. When the first UCC congress was called in 1943, I was asked to deliver a paper in the name of Ukrainian-Canadian youth. For months before the congress, every little detail was contested, from who would be the chairman to who would speak and in what order. And the speakers were not allowed to choose their own subjects, but were told what they should say. Even then there was so much distrust that people would say, "But how do we know that in this paper he is not going to say something beneficial to his organization and detrimental to ours?"

My own paper was not very nationalistic because I realized that in a time of war it was necessary to be diplomatic and to avoid stepping on people's toes. The paper was sent to John Solomon at the USRL. He rejected it because it placed too much stress on the homeland. In the view of the USRL, I had to limit myself to Ukrainian-Canadian issues and to the role of the youth in those issues, without any reference to the "old country." I refused to rewrite my speech. The UNF put pressure on me, arguing that it was better to have me speak than someone from the Catholic or Orthodox groups. It was a matter of prestige to have our own person speak, regardless of what he said.

I insisted that I would not change my speech. Finally Paul Macenko, a member of the UNF hierarchy in Winnipeg, wrote a speech, and I was urged to read it. "This is not my speech. Why should I deliver it?" I said. "Change it a little bit, but don't change the tenor, because that has been agreed upon," I was told. So I made a few changes, mostly grammatical, and in that form my speech, if it could be called that, was accepted. It consisted largely of platitudes and generalities.

The tenor of the whole UCC congress was no different. It was impressed upon the UCC by its patrons, Watson Kirkconnell and George Simpson, who were present at all the sessions, that the purpose of the congress was to assert the loyalty of Ukrainian Canadians to Canada and to offer support for the war effort.

I was studying political science and economics at the University of Toronto and teaching part-time at a Ukrainian school. From university I would get on a streetcar and hurry to the UNF hall at 300 Bathurst Street to teach. The building had once been a Ukrainian Communist hall, and the UNF had acquired it from the Custodian of Enemy Property. Osyp Nazaruk was the choir conductor and teacher, and I was the assistant teacher. Every day I taught for an hour and a half or two and then all afternoon on Saturdays.

At my father's insistence, I had started out in 1941 in first-year veterinary medicine. The sciences had been my weak subjects in school, and I didn't particularly care for medicine, but I had no choice. Europeans wanted the respectability of the medical profession, and my father gave me an ultimatum. "I pay your tuition, and so you've got to be a doctor," he said. I enrolled in medical school and was miserable. I had a squeamish stomach and gagged easily. There was no premedical course in those days, and students dissected animals in the first year. Although the carcasses were preserved in formaldehyde, a smell of rotting meat was still detectable. I would lay out a specimen and then run to the toilet to vomit. When I came home in the evening and sat down to the supper my mother had waiting for me, I thought I could smell formaldehyde in the pores of my skin even though I had scrubbed my hands on leaving the lab and on coming home. Then I would gag again.

My father was adamant that I become a doctor. He thought I was a weakling and did not understand why I could not overcome my revulsion by willpower. I quit medicine in January 1942. I was afraid to tell my father and spent the days at the UNF hall, making speeches, writing letters, teaching and taking part in plays. Every

Saturday and Sunday a play was put on, and when I was not on the stage I was in the prompter's box. Only the following fall, when I enrolled in political science, did I finally tell my father that I had dropped medicine.

At the national convention of the UNF shortly after the UCC congress in 1943, I replaced Paul Yuzyk as president of the Dominion Executive, as it was called then, of the Ukrainian National Youth Federation. The executive decided to form the *Oseredok*, or Ukrainian Cultural and Educational Centre, in Winnipeg. I was chosen as the first field representative and was sent on a lecture tour of Western Canada to promote the centre and to set up local cells that would help raise funds. I went to Regina and Saskatoon and from there to Alberta, where I met my future wife, Gloria Kupchenko. Her father, Volodymyr Kupchenko, was a powerful orator, and it was suggested that I ask him to continue the fund-raising work when it became public.

The main purpose of the *Oseredok* was publications and cultural work. The publications were later abandoned, but three or four booklets were published in 1943 and 1944. The editor was the poet Honore Ewach. The composer and choirmaster Oleksander Koshyts had arrived in Winnipeg in 1941, and the *Oseredok* engaged him to teach young people to conduct orchestras and choirs. After his death in 1944 his wife Tetiana and Paul Macenko, who was a musicologist, continued his work. Summer courses for young people in the Ukrainian language and literature were another project of the *Oseredok*, which continued for many years. My wife's father taught Ukrainian history at the courses.

As the national president of the UNYF, I also promoted the idea, which was heretical at the time, of publishing a section of *Novyi shliakh*, or *New Pathway*, in English, because many young Ukrainians in Canada did not read Ukrainian and were asking whether it made any sense to publish the paper if nobody read it. Despite all its efforts to prove its loyalty and patriotism, the UNF did not see that this was another way of showing that Ukrainians were good Canadians. But I won the argument, and *Novyi shliakh* introduced an English-language page called "Youth Speaks." I agreed to be the editor and to contribute to it.

At that time, only volunteers were being sent overseas, but general conscription had already been introduced. Exemptions were made for university students, as long as they passed their courses. Military training was compulsory at the university, and I took it for three years. Yet even officers in the reserves could not count on getting a commission in the active forces, and so I thought I would enlist if I could be assured a commission. I suppose that I still had a European background and could not imagine myself serving as a buck private with a bunch of yokels. This may have been snobbism, but I thought I had the qualifications to be at least a second lieutenant.

Paul Yuzyk had a similar notion. In 1943 he was already serving as a lance corporal with a sapper unit. At the UNF convention in conjunction with the UCC congress the highest level of the national executive debated how Yuzyk could be promoted. He urged the UNF to use its influence to get Brigadier General Trudeau – I remember the name because it is also the name of our former prime minister – the commanding officer of the military district that took in Saskatchewan, to send him to officer training school. A letter was written to Trudeau, but it brought no results and Yuzyk was never commissioned.

I made a similar effort. The officer who commanded the military district that took in southern Ontario was a brigadier named Potts. I went to see him and told him that I wanted to join the armed forces, but with an assurance that I would be commissioned. Potts thought it was terribly presumptuous of me, a "foreigner," to aspire to be an officer. I told him that I had spent my youth in Europe and knew German, Polish and Russian. Surely I could be useful somewhere? Potts replied that even his own son had joined the army as a private. I refrained from asking what rank he had now.

In the fall of 1943, after I had returned from western Canada, recruiting officers came to the University of Toronto to recruit officers for the armoured corps. The prospect was not particularly pleasing, but after some thought I put in an application. Then I got a letter from defence headquarters ordering me to report to the officers' school in Brockville, Ontario, for a physical examination.

The examinations at university had been perfunctory: the doctor put a stethoscope to my heart, gave me a short arm inspection and ordered me to bend over. In Brockville, I was thoroughly examined by a team of specialists. They found that my lungs had been damaged by the tuberculosis that I had contracted in Ukraine and said that I was unfit for service.

I concluded that the next best thing would be a job associated with the military. The newly created Department of National War Services, under General La Fleche, was looking for people who had knowledge of Slavic languages. I had left Ukraine just two years before, and my Ukrainian was very good, as were my Polish and Russian, much better than anyone else's in Canada. I applied for the job, wrote the exam, in which I got the highest mark, and started working in the fall of 1944.

The title for the position was reader, and my duties consisted of informing the government about the views of the Slavic newspapers published in Canada. I didn't know Czech, Slovak or Serbo-Croatian, but since I knew Ukrainian, Russian and Polish, I could read a Slovak or Croatian paper and get the gist. I also analyzed the sources the papers used – how much was taken from other newspapers, how much was original, how much came from the country of their origin, in short, what proportion of the contents referred to "old-country" affairs and what proportion to Canadian politics. I even measured the articles in column inches to determine the degree to which these papers were "Canadianized" or assimilated. The reports I prepared went to my own minister, the Department of External Affairs and the RCMP.

In addition, there were intelligence activities that I am not at liberty to discuss, because I took an oath for life. We wore civilian clothing, but the job was military, and although I was not aware of all the connections, I am sure that the work had something to do with Sir William Stephenson and Camp X, where saboteurs and spies were trained before being dropped behind the enemy lines. The activities in which I was involved were run by Canadians, but Canada did not have any sustained anti-nazi propaganda organization equivalent to the BBC in Britain, and the information we obtained was used by the British to wage political and psychological warfare and to undermine the morale of the German armed forces and civilian populace.

In Ottawa, I frequently saw Volodymyr Kysilevsky, or Vladimir Kaye, as he called himself in English. I had met him at the UCC congress in 1943. People were always seeking his advice. When I got to know him, I often wondered why people respected him. Ukrainians are emotional, but Kaye was always unperturbed and deliberate. He was the ultimate British civil servant, servile, loyal and more British and more monarchistic than the British themselves. He tried to ape the British and to look like an English country squire. He even affected a British accent, although he did not speak English fluently. The effect was strange beyond words. And yet what racial or cultural ties could he have had with the British monarchy? I saw him in Ottawa just a year before his death. He still spoke with that pseudo-British accent of his.

Some Anglo-Saxon – perhaps Tracy Philipps, George Simpson or Watson Kirkconnell – must have pushed Kaye onto the Ukrainian community for him to have won the influence that he enjoyed. Ukrainians will respect another Ukrainian only if an influential Anglo-Saxon says that he respects him. Kaye had that kind of respect, but I don't know how he earned it because he had never done anything for the Ukrainian cause in Canada.

Kaye may have also attained his position in the Ukrainian community because he was a civil servant. Few Ukrainians worked for the government then. When I came to Toronto in 1941 some Ukrainians told me, in tones of reverence, that their daughter was a salesgirl at Eaton's, as if a white-collar job were a tremendous accomplishment. Kaye certainly projected an image of importance that his position did not entitle him to. He talked *ex cathedra* to representatives of the UCC and never did anything to disabuse them of the notion that he was speaking for the government. Special Constable Michael Petrowsky, who worked for the RCMP, may have been equal in rank to Kaye and certainly worked in a more sensitive area, but he simply did his job and did not try to influence the course of events the way Kaye did.

In late 1944, people – I presume they were from the MI5 branch of British intelligence – came to Ottawa to look for Canadians with facility in Russian and expertise in Soviet affairs, and someone from the British High Commission asked me whether I would be interested in applying for intelligence work in England. Since I was well qualified – better qualified, I later discovered, than many of the people whom I met at St. James Square in London, where the British intelligence community had its headquarters – I applied for the job. In May 1945, when all the arrangements for my departure had been completed, including swearing an oath and signing a contract stating that I would be bound by the Official Secrets Act, I boarded a Liberator bomber and flew from Montreal, via Labrador, to Scotland. After a short stay in Edinburgh, I went to London and was there for V-E Day, when the war in Europe ended.

CHAPTER 9

THE CALL OF BLOOD

The British government, in the early days of the post-war realignment, was concerned with the administration of occupied Germany and Austria and the sharing of political and military power over the conquered areas with the USSR. During the war, the propaganda machine had worked overtime to conceal any disagreements with the Soviet Union in order not to undermine the war effort. Now realism took over, and the people in charge of national security were preparing for the possibility of Soviet expansion into central and western Europe. Austria was split off from Germany, and control commissions for both countries were set up. The Control Commission for Germany, to which I was assigned, had to consider a number of problems, from the restoration of communications, railways, health services and food distribution to relations with the Soviet Union and the German populace.

Ukrainians serving in the Canadian armed forces in Britain had met in Manchester in January 1943 to form the Ukrainian Canadian Servicemen's Club, or UCSA. After its first congress, the UCC had asked for permission to establish a Ukrainian regiment, similar to the Toronto Scottish and Irish regiments. The request was turned down. If it was granted, the authorities said, all the other ethnic groups would want their own units and the Canadian army would be weakened. Why, then, did the government permit a Ukrainian-Canadian service club? One explanation that I heard was that Ukrainians occupied a peculiar position. Roman Catholicism and Protestantism were the only religious affiliations recognized by the Canadian army. Even Jews were classified as Protestants. Since Ukrainians followed a different religious calendar, a separate organization would boost their morale by allowing them to observe their holidays.

A more serious reason may have been that even before the war both the Canadian and the British governments feared that Germany might create an independent Ukraine. Forces in Germany – particularly Canaris's intelligence service and Rosenberg's *Ostministerium* – had advocated just such a course. And it was known that Ukrainians would welcome Germany's support in gaining independence. Bohdan Panchuk and Ann Crapleve were recognized in the New Year's Honours List after the war for forming the UCSA and contributing to the morale of servicemen overseas, but opposition to the club persisted to the very end. Was the spectre of Germany's Ukrainian policy haunting Canadian political leaders when they grudgingly granted permission to establish the UCSA?

My work at the CCG at first kept me in a state of semi-confinement, and I went to the UCSA, which had moved from Manchester to 218 Sussex Gardens in Paddington, only some weeks after I arrived in London. Having read the Ukrainian press in Ottawa, I knew that the UCSA raised money and sent parcels to troops overseas. I had imagined a club-like atmosphere, but the premises struck me as spartan. Sleeping facilities consisted of narrow cots with broken springs and rough army blankets; notices were tacked up everywhere, and the place needed paint and repairs. Still, I was glad to spend my evenings and weekends there. British intelligence was swarming with former white Russians whose outlook was not compatible with my own. Although they were probably not aware of my Ukrainian nationalist sentiments, I always felt awkward and alienated at St. James Square.

In August 1945 I was involved in the formation of the Association of Ukrainians in the Polish Armed Forces. The Polish army had discriminated against Ukrainians, and many of them revealed themselves as Ukrainians only when they came to the UCSA. Although they were welcomed at the club, they could not join it because it was for Ukrainian-Canadian servicemen. So to give them a sense of self-worth we set up an organization for them and gave them office space at Sussex Gardens. At the founding meeting, Mykyta Bura became the president, and Hryhorii Drabat, an activist in the Bandera faction of the OUN, became the editor of the paper *Nash klych*, or "Our Call," to which I contributed. It was typed on our Ukrainian typewriter at Sussex Gardens and then printed on photographic paper.

Ever since the Allied landing in Normandy in 1944, Ukrainian-Canadian servicemen had been reporting to the UCSA that they had met Ukrainians on the continent. Some were in German uniforms. Others were *Ostarbeiters* who had been drafted to work in German factories and farms. Some were inmates of German concentration camps. Still others were refugees from the Soviet Union. As the war in Europe ground to an end, more information came in torrents. Long before V-E Day it was clear that as many as a million Ukrainians were living in the Third Reich, that many of them had no wish to return to Soviet-occupied Ukraine and that all of them were in dire need of help.

With the cessation of hostilities in 1945, it became apparent that the creation of an organization to help the Ukrainian refugees demanded urgent action. We discussed the problem at the UCSA, and on our initiative the Central Ukrainian Relief Bureau, or CURB, came into existence. Bohdan Panchuk became the director, and I the secretary general. When Panchuk was discharged and returned to Canada in May 1946, I succeeded him as director. I found a niche for myself at the CURB because I was stationed in London and spent much time at Sussex Gardens and because I knew Ukrainian well. Inquiries were coming from both individuals and the organizations that were springing up spontaneously in the refugees camps in Germany. Who would answer them? Crapleve knew only a few words of Ukrainian. Panchuk, who also could not write in Ukrainian, could not be secretary. And I could not be both secretary and director. The UCC in Winnpeg made the decision to use my services, and Panchuk is wrong when he asserts in *Heroes of Their Day* that he set up the operation and hired other people. Whoever happened to be there did whatever he could. Those who were there more often naturally directed the work of those who were there less often.

Members of the Allied armed forces took part in the work of the CURB when they came to London on leave. Among them were M. E. Lucyk, Michael Kapusta, Peter Smylski, Joe Romanow,

Stephen Davidovich, George Luckyj, William Byblow and Anne Cherniawsky. Vladimir de Korostovetz, D. Melnyk, Frank Martyniuk, Ann Crapleve, Helen Kozicky, P. Stefaniuk, M. Chechnita, the Reverend Michael Horoshko, the Reverend Symchych, Steve Yaworsky and Anthony Yaremovich gave valuable service. Many servicemen stationed in other parts of the United Kingdom and on the continent gave casual help. The paid clerical staff consisted of one English-language secretary and one Ukrainian secretary.

The problems we faced were of such magnitude that we needed the support of all Ukrainians in the free world, and especially of the Ukrainian Canadian Committee and the Ukrainian Congress Committee of America. When the two umbrella organizations formed relief organizations – the Ukrainian-Canadian Relief Fund and the United Ukrainian-American Relief Committee – the CURB became the outpost through which they channelled aid. At the same time the displaced persons, or DPs, as the refugees in Europe became known, were setting up local and regional relief committees in Austria and the American and British zones of Germany. The Ukrainian communities in France, Belgium, Switzerland, Italy, Argentina and Brazil also established committees. The CURB became the co-ordinating body for all of them.

I must admit, though this may sound megalomaniac, that we conceived the CURB as being a world congress of free Ukrainians. This is why we listed on our letterhead Ukrainian relief committees as far away as Argentina and Brazil. At the three conferences that we held in London and Paris, representatives of the refugee organizations stated that they wanted the CURB to be their spokesmen and to become the voice of all Ukrainians. Of course, they envisaged enlarging the CURB and including representatives of the various committees. In this respect we were *ad idem* with the European committees. Immodest though this may sound, I think we were more qualified than either the UCC or the UCCA to solve these problems. We were on the spot and knew the situation better than they did. But we lacked finances. Much as the people on the continent wanted us to provide leadership, they were not in a position to finance our work. Since we needed funding, we had to knuckle under and carry out the directives of those who gave it to us.

The UCC would not permit us to set the goals and parameters for the CURB because it claimed to represent the community. If I heard that argument once, I heard it a hundred times at meetings of the UNF, the USRL and the UCC between 1941 and the time I left for overseas. Speakers would get up on the stage and say, "Gentlemen, we are the Ukrainian parliament!" They revelled in their feeling of importance: they were the spokesmen not only for Ukrainian-Canadians, but for all Ukraine. The memoranda that were sent to the Canadian and American governments always said, "We speak not only on behalf of our communities in Canada and the United States, but on behalf of the Ukrainian nation, which cannot speak for itself." Anthony Hlynka, a Social Credit MP from Vegreville, Alberta, even made a proposal, which was ridiculed in the House of Commons, that the UCC be recognized as the representative of Ukraine at the United Nations.

In the beginning we saw material aid to the DPs as our first priority. But soon a variety of relief organizations – the International Red Cross, Caritas, CARE and UNRRA – took over the job of providing them with food, shelter and clothing. Our job was assistance in resettlement and political defence. The Ukrainian DPs were not recognized as having a nationality or ethnocultural origin of their own and were not allowed to call themselves Ukrainians. Nationality was equated with citizenship, and Ukrainians had to declare themselves by reference to their former citizenship. People who came from Bukovyna, which had been under Romania before 1940, were regarded as Romanians, and Western Ukrainians were classified as Poles. The Balts were recognized as separate nationalities even though their countries had been incorporated into the Soviet Union. Jews were recognized although Israel had not been established yet. The Ukrainians alone were denied their culture, language and national origin. I don't know where the practice originated, but documents exist to substantiate that this was a policy. Since this was a political and not a military matter, I suspect that the policy came from the Foreign Office.

At the insistence of the Communist countries an agreement was concluded prohibiting propaganda against any of the allies in the camps. In Western eyes, this meant that nazism and fascism could not be revived. The Soviets interpreted the agreement as a ban on anti-Soviet propaganda. To them, all the refugees from the Soviet Union were anti-Communist, and their refusal to go home was proof. Anything they did was anti-communist, whether it was founding a school, a newspaper, a theatre or a dance group. So the Soviets insisted that the Western allies abide by the letter, and not merely the spirit, of the agreement. The allies gave in to the demand and banned all forms of organizational life in the DP camps. Later, exceptions were made, but Ukrainians were the last to be granted these rights. While others were finally allowed to have their own organizations, the Ukrainians were still not permitted to form even apolitical cultural organizations. Thus we saw a legitimate and important role for the CURB in fighting for the civil liberties of the Ukrainian refugees.

Ukrainian-Canadian servicemen would come to London with suitcases full of letters that Ukrainians in the DP camps had asked them to forward and would ask us what to do with them. There was no civilian post then, and we used military channels to deliver the letters to the United States and Canada. In this fashion the CURB became an intermediary between Europe and North and South America, transmitting letters from the DPs to the Americas and food, medicine and clothing to the camps.

Many of the writers were seeking relatives and friends. All the Ukrainian newspapers at that time carried search columns. They would get the notices from us. Relatives who wanted to respond could do so only by writing to us in London, and we would try to forward the responses to the camps. Sending mail from Canada to London was not a problem, but how were we to get it to the continent? If the addressees were in France or Belgium, we would ask the committee in Belgium to deliver the mail. But most of the addressees were in Germany. No mail service, apart from the military postal service, was available, and no civilian trains or airlines were functioning. Like the intelligence services, we had to establish our field operatives.

In our London office we had a large map of Europe, studded with pins of various colours, which directed us to a file in which we could find the name, rank, unit and military field post address of every Ukrainian serviceman in the Canadian, American, British and Polish armed forces on the continent. Joe Romanow devised an elaborate cross-index to enable instant retrieval of information on any serviceman or civilian in a DP camp, or elsewhere in Europe and the Americas. If we got a letter for someone in Hannover, we would look at the map and the list to find a serviceman in the area, then send the letter to him through the military post and ask him to deliver it. Some letters were no doubt lost because not everyone was willing to go out of his way, but most reached their destinations.

A further monumental task – a census aimed at getting accurate data on all the Ukrainian DPs – was undertaken. A questionnaire was prepared and mimeographed copies were sent to all the DP camps and to refugees living outside the camps. Despite the difficult post-war conditions and the prevailing mood of fear, uncertainty and despair, most of the questionnaires were filled out and returned to the CURB. They furnished a clear picture of the refugees as to age, occupation, education, place of origin, relatives in North America and preference in emigration.

The CURB also provided medical and legal aid to the refugees. Such dentists as Drs. Lucyk, Smylski and Michael Kapusta not only helped maintain lines of communication while they were stationed in Germany, but spent all their free time helping Ukrainian DPs, offering their professional skills and supplying the medical and dental clinics in the camps with much needed supplies.

Through Kaye and Davidovich, who had headed Ukrainian information bureaus in London before the war, as well as Danylo Skoropadsky and Vladimir de Korostovetz, the CURB had access to Conservative and Labour MPs and peers who had influence on the formulation of British policy towards the refugees. On several occasions, questions about that policy were raised in both houses. We then reproduced the relevant portion of Hansard for our committees and newspapers in the United States and Canada. Other influential friends were cultivated by members of the CURB who joined British clubs, where additional contacts were made and political issues were often resolved.

In 1947, at the request of Metropolitan Polikarp of the Ukrainian Autocephalic Orthodox Church in Germany, I became involved in negotiations with the Church of England. The Ukrainian church, which had been reborn under German occupation, was concerned to establish that it was different from the Ukrainian Orthodox church established by Metropolitan Lypkivsky in 1920. All the Orthodox bishops in Ukraine had been Russians. When the Ukrainians wanted to declare their independence from the patriarch of Moscow, the Russian bishops refused to consecrate a Ukrainian bishop. Lypkivsky was elevated to bishop by the early Christian practice of the laying on of hands, and he in turn consecrated other bishops. The Russians argued that the church was not legitimate because it had violated the apostolic succession that traces from Christ to the present. Even other Ukrainian churches contemptuously referred to the autocephalic bishops as "self-consecrated."

The Bishop of Chichester had been designated to handle relations with other churches, and I went to see him several times. The material that I brought to him from Polikarp showed that the new autocephalic church had the right of succession because Dionisius, the head of the Polish Orthodox Church, had consecrated a Ukrainian bishop, and Dionisius had been consecrated by the patriarch of Jerusalem, who had apostolic succession. One result of the contact with the Church of England was that it agreed to bring Orthodox students over to England and to provide financial support for them while they were studying. In my conversations with the bishop I also brought up the plight of the DPs. He became one of the most dedicated champions of their cause and spoke out against forced repatriation in the House of Lords.

At a DP conference I learned about a group of Ukrainian

scientists who had studied the production of a rubber substitute. Natural rubber came only from Malaysia, and every country, Germany included, was desperately trying to find a substitute for rubber, which is required in great amounts by the war industry. The Soviets had put the scientists to work on the development of a rubber substitute derived from chandrilla, a plant that grows in the steppes of Ukraine. When the war broke out, they were not evacuated east for some reason and were put to work for the Germans. At the end of the war the scientists wrote to me at the CURB, outlining their history and asking to be resettled as a group because they wanted to continue their research.

Armed with letters of introduction from Vladimir de Korostovetz, I went to Dublin to meet the Irish prime minister, the attorney general and the apostolic nuncio to discuss the admission of the Ukrainian refugees to Ireland. I had already spent my leaves in Dublin. Ireland was a good place to visit because it had been neutral during the war. Entry visas were not required; food was not rationed, and even milk and steaks were available. I liked the Irish and their country. They were very politicized and reminded me of Ukrainian nationalists in the fervency of their actions and beliefs. As soon as I got off the boat after crossing the Irish Sea, they would start telling me what an injustice the British had done them when they took away the six counties. Although they were thought of as being insular, Catholic and intolerant, the Irish had opened their doors to the Huguenots when they were being persecuted in France. I used this as a wedge and told the Irish that they had a reputation for helping persecuted people. Now they had a chance to help victims of Stalinism. The government was favourably disposed, but no Ukrainian refugees emigrated to Eire. Everyone preferred Canada and the United States.

The gravest problem that the CURB faced was the prevention of forced repatriation to the Soviet Union. The implementation of the Yalta agreement led to Dantesque scenes of horror in which former Soviet citizens and those alleged to be such resisted repatriation with all the means at their disposal, including mass suicide. Readers of Aleksandr Solzhenitsyn's *Gulag Archipelago* now know what was in store for all those who were repatriated.

·

Even Red Army soldiers who had been captured by the Germans were incarcerated for ten years or more in the concentration camps of the Soviet Gulag.

Both the Foreign Office and the War Office often referred repatriation matters to the CCG, and I am certain that the decision to repatriate anyone was political. Nikolai Tolstoy's *Victims of Yalta* and Nicholas Bethell's *The Last Secret* leave no doubt that a few Foreign Office officials interpreted the Yalta agreement as providing for the use of force even though the text made no mention of it. We also know that many commanders in the field, of whom the foremost was Lord Alexander, the former governor general, resisted demands to lend a hand in repatriating Soviet nationals in the areas under their command. Thus the Foreign Office was by and large not sympathetic to Ukrainian concerns. Yet if we remember that the head of the Soviet desk at that time was Kim Philby, we shall not be surprised that the policy makers at the Foreign Office made such decisions.

The simplest and often most effective way of preventing forced repatriation was to pass off Ukrainians from the Soviet Union as Western Ukrainians. The Yalta agreement bound the allies to repatriate citizens of the USSR as it was constituted before 1 September 1939. This meant that people from Western Ukraine, Western Belorussia and the Baltic countries, which had been incorporated into the USSR as a result of the Molotov-Ribbentrop pact, were not considered Soviet citizens and were not subject to repatriation. Panchuk and I therefore issued "to whom it may concern" letters on the UCSA or CURB letterhead. We would state that we knew so-and-so had been born in, or had been a resident of, such-and-such a place in Western Ukraine, and then sign our names, ranks and units. Such letters were hardly legal, but they served as surprisingly effective passports and were often accepted without question by the British liaison officers who accompanied every Soviet repatriation commission in the British zones of Austria and Germany. At times, we obtained identity documents from the Polish Military Mission in Paris. In other cases, Mr. Popovich of the Ukrainian Relief Committee in France issued documents. His association with French trade unions made his task easier, because pro-Soviet sentiments were strong in post-war France and documents were difficult to obtain. The Ukrainian Red Cross in Geneva issued blank identity documents, and Ukrainian priests – there was at least one in every Ukrainian DP camp – made out baptismal certificates in which the place of birth, and often the surname as well, were false.

These measures did not work in every case, and it was not possible to issue new identity papers for all the Eastern Ukrainians who did not want go home. The very practice of repatriation by force had to be stopped. We tried everything from arguing with the government to complaining to the press that repatriation was inconsistent with democratic principles. Even before the CURB was born, the UCSA submitted memoranda to political and military leaders. The CURB stepped up this approach and sent additional memoranda to the British government, the International Red Cross and the UNRRA. And Panchuk and I wrote letters to British parliamentarians, churchmen, writers and journalists, explaining why the DPs did not want to go "home."

Mike Kapusta was an on-the-spot defender of those Ukrainians who were to be repatriated by force. Although he was never a member of any repatriation commission, his uniform enabled him to intervene without anyone questioning his right to do so. Word would spread that a Soviet repatriation commission had appeared and refugees were being rounded up, and there would be Kapusta, protesting, arguing and providing evidence of citizenship on behalf of the threatened. God alone knows how many people he saved. And although he was the most prominent, he was by no means the only one engaged in this activity.

In February 1946, the CURB managed to present the case against forced repatriation to a session of the United Nations General Assembly that took place in London. Just before the assembly was convened Peter Smylski and I went to see where the session would be held. It was a little after five o'clock when we got there, and most of the staff had left. We discovered that there was no security: the doors were open, and perhaps because we were in uniform we were able to enter without being challenged. As we wandered through the offices, I spotted a pile of mimeographed lists of delegates to the session with their London addresses. It took only a second to slip a copy under my tunic. Still unmolested, Smylski and I walked out. This was Saturday evening, and the first plenary session was starting on Monday. We went straight to Steve Davidovich's flat, and the three of us spent the better part of the night composing a memorandum. Back at 218 Sussex Gardens, Panchuk made a few last-minute changes in the text. We spent Sunday typing, mimeographing and mailing the memorandum to the delegates.

At the plenary session, Eleanor Roosevelt, the head of the United States delegation, made a speech in which, drawing heavily on our memorandum, she denounced forced repatriation, announced that the United States would not help return people to the Soviet Union and urged all countries concerned to discontinue the practice. We were naturally very pleased because we thought that this would be the end of forced repatriation. We distributed our memorandum, Mrs. Roosevelt's speech and the subsequent reports in the British press to all the Canadian newspapers, and the matter gained much publicity. The Soviets changed their tactics and began accusing all refugees of war crimes and demanding their return without proof of guilt, and incidents of forced repatriation occurred occasionally even after the United Nations adopted the resolution. Nonetheless, our memorandum to the United Nations was our crowning achievement. If we had done nothing more, our whole effort would have been justified.

The sequel to the story is interesting. At a cocktail party before the session, Mrs. Roosevelt mentioned to Tracy Philipps that she had received the memorandum. She was dismayed to learn about the forced repatriation of former Soviet citizens, but she wondered whether the facts were true and the signatories represented the bodies they professed to speak for. Philipps reassured her on both points, and she then made use of the memorandum. Philipps later related the conversation to Watson Kirkconnell, who in turn told the story to Smylski.

I cannot even begin to enumerate all the memoranda, letters and interventions expended to save the Galicia division, except to say that at certain times it was but a hair's breadth away from being shipped to the USSR notwithstanding the non-Soviet citizenship of its members. At Potsdam Stalin specifically demanded the return of the division. No other military formation, the Vlasov army included, was ever singled out in this way. It was primarily through the efforts of the CURB and the actions undertaken vis-a-vis their governments by the UCC and the UCCA that the Galicia division was not handed over to the Soviet military authorities, although it was not possible to prevent this in the case of the Ukrainian POWs who had served in the nationality units of the Wehrmacht.

Ukrainian personnel were housed at the POW camp in Kirkham, Lancashire. We got wind of the camp, but try as we would we could not gain admission to it. Finally the War office conceded that, under the provisions of the Geneva Convention, POWs were entitled to spiritual succor and granted permission for a priest and a precentor to conduct a service for the POWs, but not to meet them. Half a loaf was better than none, and I had no difficulty in persuading the Reverend Perridon, the Catholic priest of the Ukrainian parish in Paris and "apostolic visitator" to Great Britain, to come to England for this purpose. Perridon was of Dutch origin, and his Ukrainian was limited, but he was a supporter of the "Byzantine school," which was in favour of de-Latinizing the Eastern rite. I recalled that under the great Metropolitan Ilarion in Kievan Rus' learned laymen were invited to preach in his cathedral. Perridon agreed that the Eastern church had known such a practice and that I could deliver the sermon.

In Kirkham, we were met by the priest of the local Anglican church, which had been offered to us for the service. The commandant of the POW camp, a British army officer, met us at the vicar's residence and took us for dinner at the officers' mess. He was a kindly man, well disposed to his "boys," who gave him no trouble and were hard-working and co-operative. Over dinner I discussed matters close to my heart: the danger that the POWs might be deported by force to the Soviet Union. The commandant seemed sympathetic and agreed with our views on this subject, including the proposition that the Yalta agreement did not require handing over those who had been Polish citizens before the outbreak of the war. Nevertheless, he made no promises.

In the evening, the Ukrainian POWs were marched in under guard from the sugar-beet farm to the church. After he had read the Gospel, Perridon announced that he would hear confessions while I delivered the sermon. I tried to lift the POWs' morale and keep their hopes burning. Then I went on to describe the CURB and its aims, especially in the area of preventing forced repatriation, and dwelt on the loophole provided in the Yalta agreement by the definition of citizenship as the basis for repatriation. I tried to make myself clear without crossing the t's and dotting the i's. To make the point even clearer, I recounted how Mike Kapusta had been able to thwart the Soviet repatriation teams. There was not much of a Christian message in my sermon, but I might have rendered the POWs a greater service by showing them a way out of their predicament.

The story had a happy ending. In 1978, I addressed the Ukrainian Professional and Business Club of Waterloo, Wellington and Perth, Ontario, and related the story of my sermon in Kirkham. Afterwards Volodymyr Hasiy, who was now living in Guelph, approached to tell me that he had been at the POW camp in Kirkham. A Soviet repatriation team had visited the camp and interviewed the prisoners. They all claimed Polish citizenship. The commandant would not permit the Soviet officers to interrogate the prisoners at length. Only one or two got mixed up in their geography and were taken away. The rest were transported to a camp in Germany. The commandant in Kirkham had already hinted what they should do there. They stole out of the camp and disappeared by blending in with the civilian DPs.

Many of the letters that we received at the CURB were pleas for assistance. The propaganda here in Canada pictured the DPs as hungry, barefoot and unclothed, and some of the people who wrote to us did ask for material help. But most wanted to know what awaited them and where they would resettle. And they often wanted to report that they were not simply statistics, but human beings with experiences that they wanted to share. Much of the information in this category was political, especially information about what had happened in Ukraine during the war years, when all contact with Western Europe and North America had been cut off, and everybody had to be brought up to date as to what had happened, especially with regard to the UPA, the UHVR and the "legal" Ukrainian structures under German occupation.

We soon realised that if our fight against forced repatriation were to be successful, we would have to win over the politicians, the press and the public. With a few notable exceptions, people in Britain were abysmally ignorant of "the Ukrainian question," i.e., the political history of Ukraine and its struggle for freedom. They did not even know whether it was located in Europe, Africa or Asia. In addition, the tsarist Russians and their descendants who influenced British public opinion and government policy were hostile to Ukrainians and even denied their existence. The Polish government in exile was successful in branding any attempt to put forth the Ukrainian nationalist point of view as being inspired by the Germans. The Soviets charged that the DPs refused to return because they were nazi collaborators or war criminals who were afraid of facing justice. The British public, which was used to regular trials with judges, lawyers and juries, found that explanation plausible. And American GIs and British Tommies, who were anxious to go home on the first available transport, simply could not understand why the Ukrainians slashed their wrists to avoid being sent home and often used their rifle butts to help Soviet soldiers round up recalcitrant refugees and ship them off on Red Army trucks to the Soviet zone.

We were thus behind the eight ball. A handful of us were trying to save hundreds of thousands of people and were confronted with the might of the Soviet military, diplomatic and propaganda apparatus and the Yalta Treaty, signed by the United States, Britain and the Soviet Union. We refuted Soviet propaganda and tried to prevent repatriation by showing what had happened in Ukraine: the UPA had waged an underground struggle against both the Soviets and the Germans. Much was made about the French underground, but the UPA was the biggest and best organized underground resistance in any country during the

Second World War. The French Maquis, by comparison, were numerically weak and were not popular with their countrymen. Most of the French supported Petain and the Vichy government. It was only when De Gaulle came to power after the war that the French tried to absolve their guilt by magnifying the resistance that had taken place.

Any occupation obviously has to form an apparatus to administer the occupied territory. It cannot put its own people everywhere and has to make use of local people in running the railways or the postal service, for example. Are you a collaborator if you work in such a non-political capacity, providing a service to your own people? Thus everything depends on the definition of collaboration.

Some people may have been forced to work with the Gestapo, and a few may even have volunteered to work with it. I would call that person a collaborator. But I never heard of any. And that was on a lower level. There was no one on a higher level because there was no organization sufficiently important to be in any kind of partnership with the Germans. To the credit of Ukraine, I do not think that it produced a Quisling. There was no collaboration on the scale of Marshall Petain and the Vichy government in France.

There was no divergence of opinion between Panchuk and myself in this respect. We realized that we had to educate the British public and to explain who Ukrainians were, what they wanted and why they were opposed to the Communist system. To do that we had to set out the material. We also thought that it was our obligation to inform our own people in North and South America about what happened in Ukraine. We therefore subscribed to a clipping service and set up the Ukrainian Information Service as an adjunct to the CURB. Once a week we would receive a big package of clippings from the British press with references to Ukraine or Ukrainians. Using the information made available by the clipping service, we fed supplementary information to the press, wrote letters to the editors and tried to influence our British friends to counter unfavourable reports. In return for room and board at the UCSA, Dmytro Dontsov went through the clippings and prepared a weekly review of the British press that we sent to

Ukrainian newspapers in Canada and the United States. That was a useful service, and it would be interesting to locate copies of the review because it would shed much light on the activities of the CURB. Unfortunately, as Panchuk and I learned later, few of these reports were published in our press in North America. Our effort was all but wasted.

I first went to the continent in the winter of 1945-1946. A driver with an open jeep met me when I landed at the Hook of Holland. I had with me only a trench coat, and the British major in command told the driver to take a case of schnapps to keep me warm. The schnapps was the immediate post-war product and tasted like wood alcohol. I drink very little, and I think the driver drank more of the schnapps than I did. There was only light military traffic on the highways, so I did not worry about getting into an accident. From Holland we drove to Belgium, where I met the Ukrainian Committee. In Paris I met the Ukrainians who were grouped around the Ukrainian church on the Boulevard Saint-Germaine. They included Hetmanites, Petliurites and people from the old and new emigrations.

From Paris my driver and I went to Normandy, where I interviewed a German colonel who was being held at the prisoner-of-war camp in Brest, and then to a place near Kiel on the North Sea coast, where I interrogated General Kurt Maier, the only German charged by the Canadian government as a war criminal. The allegation was that his unit had shot Canadian prisoners of war. At his trial he was exonerated.

Whenever I visited the Ukrainian DP camps in Germany, I met people whom I had known in Western Ukraine and in whom I had absolute confidence. I was still trying to find out what had happened in the Ukrainian nationalist movement during the war, and when I talked to members of either faction of the OUN I listened, weighed the evidence and made decisions only after I had all the facts. If I was not certain of something, I would ask both sides for confirmation and then compare the answers. I must say that the only corroboration I found was in the documents that the Banderites gave to me – UPA directives and resolutions of the nationalist congresses, particularly of the one at which the

Ukrainian Supreme Liberation Council, or UHVR, was founded. The UHVR had been set up in Ukraine in 1944 as an underground government. It governed the UPA and ran the OUN. On 2 December 1945, I was appointed "plenipotentiary representative" of the UHVR in Great Britain. My job was to apprise influential people in Great Britain of what had happened in Ukraine – the underground struggle, the resistance, the aspirations of the Ukrainian people – and to act as the spokesman of struggling and fighting Ukraine.

As the *terenovyi providnyk,* or resident, of the OUN for England I attended an OUN conference in Munich in November 1946. Stepan Bandera, whom I met for the first time at the conference, had become almost a demi-god. You expect a person who has a heroic reputation to be heroic in physical appearance. I was dismayed to discover that Bandera was small, balding and not in the least imposing. We talked about building up the OUN and its affiliated organizations in Britain. The membership was small, but we expected that Ukrainian refugees would eventually settle in the country. We did not know that the Galicia division would be resettled in England and membership would leap.

Although I had been born in Canada, the other members of the OUN accepted me as an equal because I had belonged to the organization in Ukraine and had direct knowledge of the West. The leadership of the free world had not been decided yet, but it was obviously going to be exercised either by Britain or by the United States. And I was the only authority on both countries. Thus my main role was to provide expertise and guidance in formulating future policies. As a Canadian, I was influenced by the education I had received and was a bit of an Anglophile. And I had lived in London for almost a year and a half, had met many English people and thought that I knew them well. I truly believed – and told the Munich assembly as much – that Britain would emerge as the leader of the free world. The United States was not qualified – and did not want – to lead the free world and would retreat into isolation, as it had done after the First World War.

Many DPs stayed on in the camps because they expected that the Western powers would go to war with the Soviet Union. Since then it has become public knowledge that Churchill contemplated the possibility of war with the Soviet Union, to the extent that he gave orders not to destroy German arms but to oil and put them away in case the Germans had to be rearmed as an ally. I cannot pretend that the intelligence sources to which I had access were of the highest level, but the information I saw never dismissed such a possibility. Thus when the OUN asked for my opinion, I said that many serious people thought that the Soviets would push and push until the West would be forced to draw a line and to say that armed conflict would result if they crossed it. As a result, the OUN tended to orientate itself to Britain. Curiously enough, when Mykola Lebed and some supporters of the UHVR split off from the Banderites, the new faction took a pro-American point of view. I must admit that it was right and I was wrong.

The consequence of my attendance at the conference was closer collaboration with the British and the supplying of personnel for parachute drops of agents into the Carpathians. One man who was dropped was my bodyguard in Munich. "Dmytro," as he was known in the organization, would pick me up at the flat where I was staying, take me to the conference and then join the other body-guards to stand watch by the door. After he was dropped into the Carpathians, he was taken prisoner, brainwashed and put on public display. The only person he knew in the OUN was me. That's why the Communists started after me. They knew very early who I was, and yet they were still hounding and beating Ostafiichuk to make him tell them where I was hiding.

Early in 1946, the CURB organized a fact-finding mission to the continent by the Reverend Wasyl Kushnir, the president of the UCC. I distinctly remember that visit. For some reason, the Ukrainian-Canadian newspapers called the UCSA a "canteen." In military usage, there were two kinds of canteens: wet canteens, which were bars, and dry canteens, which were run by the Salvation Army and did not serve alcohol. But the word canteen was associated with liquor, and I don't understand why the club in Sussex Gardens, which was dry, was called a canteen. The name led Ukrainian Canadians to believe that they were giving their boys overseas a good time. When Kushnir arrived at the club, he said, "Well, where's the drink, fellows?" Liquor was rationed and hard to come by, but John Swystun went to an officer's mess and managed to get a bottle of Scotch.

Once he had had a drink, Kushnir began talking about his "mission" in Europe. He said that he was carrying the key to what he called "solidarity," and that was the formula under which the UCC had come into existence. Kushnir was obsessed with the idea of solidarity. We have to be united, he said. But the unity that he had conceived was a mechanical one that permitted no dissent or criticism. Such unity did not come about by organic growth, but was imposed. A structure was clamped together, and content was poured into a rigid, unchangeable form.

Then Kushnir called meetings in Europe, although he could not get over there. At that time I already had sympathies for the Conservative Party. I knew George Drew, the premier of Ontario, and when he became leader of the federal party I ran for Parliament in 1953. In Toronto there was a Ukrainian Conservative Club, which Hultay, the president of the eastern Canadian executive of the UNF, had formed. Drew always came to Ukrainian affairs, and Ukrainian issues received much publicity because of this. The conservative *Toronto Telegram* was particularly sympathetic to Ukrainian questions, and my wife's father had run as a Conservative under Bennett in 1935 in Alberta.

On my arrival in London, I had paid a courtesy call on R. B. Bennett, the former Canadian prime minister, who lived on the outskirts of London and had an office in the High Commission at Canada House. As the honorary president of the Canadian Red Cross overseas and a peer, Bennett had considerable influence. When he tried to find out who I was, I told him about my connections with his former party. That opened the door for me. Whenever there was any problem, I could count on getting assistance either from Bennett or from the Canadian Red Cross.

Now, when Kushnir needed permission to go to the continent, I took him to Canada House and introduced him to Lord Bennett. Norman Robertson, who was the Canadian high commissioner in London, could not be called a friend of the Ukrainian cause, but Kushnir received permission to go to the continent. The High

Commission had no one to facilitate the trip, and Panchuk, who was stationed in the British zone, got a jeep and two weeks' leave and drove Kushnir around to the various camps.

Being a Ukrainian Catholic priest, Kushnir was able to go to Rome and through the offices of Bishop Buchko went to Rimini, where the Galicia division was interned. At other times the Ukrainian DPs themselves managed to get him from one place to another. Dressed in civilian clothes, Kushnir could pass as a DP and visit the camps. Once, when he was cold, he borrowed an expensive coat with an astrakhan collar and an ermine lining. "Look at what I have!" he said when he came back to London. He took the coat to Canada, and then the owner wrote to ask, "Where is the coat I lent the Reverend Doctor Kushnir? Do I have to give my coat to a person who has ostensibly come to help me?" It was a bitter letter, and we were all embarrassed.

Another example of Kushnir's greed involved an organization of writers and artists called MUR, or *Mystetskyi ukrainskyi rukh,* which was formed in Regensburg in the American zone. Each artist donated one of his better paintings to the Ukrainian community in Canada. Kushnir took the paintings, perhaps a dozen in all, to London and then to Winnipeg. Eventually *MUR* wrote to the bureau to say that it had presented the paintings to the Ukrainian community. *MUR* had not been given confirmation that they had been received and wanted to know where they would be exhibited. When I came back to Canada in 1947, Kushnir invited me to his house. The paintings were hanging on his walls.

Kushnir was a sneaky, underhanded, smooth-talking fellow. He would use honeyed words and at the same time plot to stab you in the back. He was also materialistic and acquisitive, not at all likeable or worthy of respect. And there was a flavour of messianism about him. He was a hero. He was carrying the key of consolidation and unification that would provide the solution to the Ukrainian problem. Whether he voiced the threat or not, it was always implied that the DPs had better toe the line if they wanted help in resettlement.

When Kushnir visited Europe, he was more concerned with political problems than relief work. He was afraid that new people who held different beliefs would come to Canada and disrupt the UCC, which he had made into a comfortable boat. Both Kushnir and the five organizations that had been members from the beginning wanted the UCC to stay in placid waters and were unwilling to share it with other passengers. The question, then, was how to integrate the displaced persons into the existing structure.

Kushnir's answer was to transplant the concept of the UCC, and he went to Europe to set up a structure that would ignore the organizations that had come into being in Ukraine or in the DP camps and to establish a completely artificial structure, the *Koordy natsiinyi ukrainskyi komitet,* or Coordinating Ukrainian Committee, which even had the same initials as the *Komitet ukraintsiv Kanada,* or Ukrainian Canadian Committee, in order to destroy the hegemony of the Bandera faction of the OUN.

That hegemony – or even monopoly – had not been imposed by terror, as some people said, but by numerical and organizational superiority. The Banderites had managed to establish an organization that covered all of Western Europe. Unable to annihilate them, their opponents could only try to disarm them by resurrecting all kinds of organizations and giving each one an equal voice, regardless of its size or popularity in the community. Kushnir managed to resuscitate about twenty different parties, some of which had not existed for decades. The Banderites, who represented 80 per cent of the people, were suddenly in the minority.

Stephen Davidovich was a captain in the artillery who had been a member of the UNF in Canada and then worked for the Ukrainian Information Bureau in London before the war. When I was going overseas, Kossar told me that he was disappointed that Davidovich had moved away from the UNF and suggested that I look him up and re-establish a connection. I discovered that Davidovich had become less partisan and developed a wider vision. He was extremely able, and I greatly admired him. He had been graduated from university *summa cum laude* in the rather esoteric field of industrial management, which was quite unusual for Ukrainians, who usually studied to become doctors, dentists or school teachers. Having been in England since 1936, Davidovich had met many people, developed contacts with the government and become quite sophisticated. As with so many other able people, the community was unable to tap his talents. I got to know Danylo Skoropadsky very well and had much respect for him. He was the son of Pavlo Skoropadsky, the former *hetman* of Ukraine. I was particularly impressed by Danylo's non-partisan attitude. Although he was a pretender to the throne, he had no illusions about becoming the crowned head of a Ukrainian state. In one conversation that I had with him, he said that he would recognize any independent Ukrainian state and admitted that the chances of a monarchical government being established were rather remote. He was a Ukrainian patriot in the sense that he worked for the ideal of freedom and independence. In 1946-1947, the Hetmanites formed an alliance with Bandera's OUN. The most conservative wing of the Ukrainian political spectrum was the only party that supported the underground military struggle waged against the Germans and the Soviets by the UPA.

Vladimir de Korostovetz had served as a Russian diplomat before the Revolution and then became a journalist and political lobbyist in Berlin and London and an aide to Skoropadsky. I never liked him as much as I did Skoropadsky. For one thing, he spoke no Ukrainian. For another, my outlook was coloured by the opinions of others. Both Kaye, with whom I often discussed Ukrainian affairs in Ottawa, and Davidovich made deprecatory remarks about Korostovetz. In his relations with me, however, Korostovetz was always above-board and reliable, and I could work with him. Unlike some people, he readily shared his contacts and freely offered help whenever I needed it.

I remember how Korostovetz came to the CURB one day, just after the Admiralty had retained him to lecture on Soviet affairs to naval officers in Hamburg and Kiel and had given him the rank of a commander in the Royal Navy. Korostovetz had received a uniform, and he asked me whether it was permissible to wear his Legion of Honour with the uniform. He also wanted to know whom he should see in the DP camps in Hamburg, Kiel and Bremerhaven. He did useful anti-communist work there. This is significant because, despite their professions of love and friendship, the British were aware of the true nature of Soviet policies.

I was impressed with Tracy Philipps, who was sophisticated and knowledgeable, a gentleman in the English sense of the word. He may not have said much, but he always said it correctly. Philipps gave me considerable help when I was involved in setting up the CURB. When I needed advice on whom to contact, for example, he would give me inside information and provide recommendations. He sponsored me to membership in the Royal Automobile Club. Philipps also belonged to the Travellers Club, which was just across the street, and I occasionally lunched with him at one or the other club. I flatter myself by thinking that Philipps sponsored me for membership because he liked me. I suppose he also knew what kind of work I was involved in and felt a kinship. And he knew that my interests were more than narrowly Ukrainian-Canadian and that I had lived in Ukraine under Soviet rule.

During my school days in Western Ukraine reverence for the leaders of the OUN had been instilled in me. To me they were almost god-like. Dmytro Andrievsky was the first member of the *Provid ukrainskykh natsionalistiv,* or Leadership of the Ukrainian Nationalists, the Melnykite executive, whom I met. When I came to him with a note from Kossar stating that I was entitled to the fullest confidence, Andriewsky immediately accepted me as a member of the OUN and started telling me what was happening in Ukraine. But I already knew people who were directly involved in those events and was receiving letters from some of them. And here a fellow who had lived abroad since the end of the First World War was telling me about events in Ukraine. I had respected Andrievsky as a leader of the OUN. Now I discovered that he was not a man of integrity, honesty and character. He manipulated people and twisted the truth to serve his purposes. He accused people of being partisan, but he displayed more partisanship than any of the people whom he accused.

A case in point is that of two fellows who were interned in Spain. We learned from Polish military intelligence that a Ukrainian organization had sent two emissaries to the Western allies. A high-ranking officer who had served with the Spanish volunteer division on the Eastern front had arranged safe passage for them. They were apprehended and interned at Miranda del Ebro in Spain because their protector had been killed and could not vouch for them. The *Pax Romana* was holding a world congress in London in August 1945. Joe Romanow and I told the head of the Spanish delegation, Professor Ruiz Jimenez, about our concern for the two interned Ukrainians. Jimenez introduced us to the Spanish minister to the Court of St. James. Both Jimenez and the minister promised that they would do what they could to help.

When Andrievsky came to England, I showed him the intelligence report and asked whether he knew anything about the two men. "If you write to them," Andrievsky said to me, "ask them if they know 'Poltavskyi.'" That was his *nom de guerre* in the organization. I wrote a letter to the two men and sent it by the Spanish diplomatic pouch to Madrid. In their reply, they made no reference to "Poltavskyi." I showed the letter to Andrievsky. "They're obviously Banderites because they don't know me," he said. "Let them rot in the concentration camp." With assistance from Jimenez and the Spanish minister, the two men were eventually released. They turned out to be members of Andrievsky's Melnyk faction. He had jumped to a conclusion and would have let his men rot in a concentration camp. Any illusions I may still have had about him were destroyed. He would tell me that I was not running things objectively, but if he came to power he would only help his own.

Andrievsky was put on salary at the CURB and stayed there until he was transferred to the UCRF. He obtained his position through the intervention of the UNF in Canada and the ODWU in the United States. They wanted their own man in a position where he could make sure that only those whom they favoured would receive assistance, and they wanted to give Andrievsky a livelihood. He had lived on his organization's dole all his life. Before the war, the OUN had been able to support him, but when it split in two, the decimated Melnyk faction could obtain funds only from its supporters in the United States and Canada. Why use UNF funds when Andrievsky could be put on the payroll of an all-

Ukrainian organization such as the UCRF or the CURB? He certainly did nothing to promote welfare or relief, and he never did any organizational or secretarial work.

Dmytro Dontsov had been active in Ukrainian affairs since the turn of the century. Persecuted by the tsarist government, he fled to Galicia in 1908. In 1922 he began editing the influential intellectual monthly *Literaturno-naukovyi visnyk*. At the end of the war, when he was in France, the Soviets included his name on a list of anti-communist leaders whom they wanted apprehended and delivered into their hands. Absent-minded, impractical and no longer young, Dontsov was too proud to change his name and go underground. I thought it was imperative to rescue him, especially since the situation in France was dangerous. Many of the people in the Resistance were Stalinists; the government was pro-Soviet, and the Soviets could count on its co-operation in apprehending Dontsov.

We therefore decided to get him out of France. I cannot reveal the method we used to get him into England because it was illegal. Then, by making a tremendous effort and calling on all our friends in the government and the House of Commons, we managed to legitimize his status in England. When Andrievsky reported to Winnipeg that Dontsov sympathized with the Banderites, the UCC began to complain that Dontsov was staying at Sussex Gardens. It was the same double standard that Andrievsky had applied to the two fellows in the Spanish internment camp. If he had been threatened (and the Soviets would certainly have been glad to get their hands on him), Andrievsky would have been the first to demand protection. Everyone else could rot.

Andrievsky had another reason for holding a grudge against Dontsov. Once, while I was gone from London, Andrievsky went into my room at the CURB and searched my belongings. Dontsov caught him reading letters to me from Lebed that the secretaries had put in my room. Andrievsky tried to make a joke of it. "I have to keep an eye on the political opposition and find out what these Banderites are up to," he said. Dontsov told me what had happened when I got back. I was livid. This was a breach of civilized behaviour. A guest of the CURB had gone into my private quarters and had opened my mail. And then he had passed on the information to Panchuk and the UCC in Winnipeg, who had not known about my ties with the UHVR. Andriewsky's reaction was one of absolute cynicism. Eventually, this denunciation led to my being forced out of the CURB.

We could provide Dontsov only with a temporary residence permit in England, and it became necessary to resettle him in a country where he could be of further service to the Ukrainian community. So Yevhen Liakhovych, who was a great friend of Dontsov, helped to get him into the United States. The Communists were still hounding Dontsov and calling him an ideologue of nazism and fascism. Walter Winchell, the muckraking columnist and radio commentator, picked this up and viciously attacked Dontsov. This created problems for Dontsov, and it was felt that he would have to leave the United States. We got in touch with his old friend Yurii Rusov, who had settled in Montreal and was teaching ichthyology at the university, and Dontsov finally managed to come to Canada and to get a job as a part-time lecturer in Ukrainian literature.

My service with the CURB had a bizarre ending. Panchuk had returned to Canada in May 1946, and I had become the director of the CURB. When he came back to London in October, he showed me a directive entitled "Canadian Veterans' Relief Team and Special Relief Mission to Ukrainian Refugees, Displaced Persons and Victims of War in Western Europe." The directive, which was written in Canada and dated 6 October 1946, outlined the sponsoring bodies, the purpose of the mission, the resources and the personnel. In this schema, Panchuk was listed as the director of the relief team and the CURB, Yaremovich as the assistant director and field representative, I as second assistant director and correspondence secretary, Ann Crapleve as honorary treasurer and accountant, and Anne Panchuk as welfare officer and senior clerk and stenotypist.

I was astounded when I saw the scheme because nobody had fired me or asked me to resign as director. The only official notification I had from the UCC was a statement informing me that Panchuk and the team were going to the continent and that

Panchuk would be head of the mission, which would co-operate with the CURB. It was implied, therefore, that the team would work on the continent and I would remain with the CURB. I said that I could not accept the scheme and was going back to Canada. Nothing was said about my being fired. This illustrates the Byzantine fashion in which business was done.

Panchuk did offer me a position with the team, but I turned it down. He attributed this to the fact that it was a demotion, but I was fed up with the way things had been going, especially with the UIS. It was impossible to work when people kept changing their minds about what we were supposed to be doing. And I could no longer afford to stay in London. Panchuk later wrote that he found some documents and confronted me with them, but this is a fabrication. After my experience with Andrievsky I kept my room locked, and either Andrievsky gave material to Panchuk or they picked the lock and entered my room. There I kept blank letterheads from the UHVR. Panchuk reported this with great glee to the UCC, sending them a copy and attesting that it had been printed in Britain on British paper and that therefore I must have been responsible. He also jumped to the conclusion that political material was being sent out from the CURB. But I had been very meticulous about sending things out under a different name and from a different address.

In a cable on 6 February 1946 the UCC had stated that it had appointed me secretary general of the CURB and would pay me a monthly salary of $250. Two days later the UCC made the same promise in a letter. At the urging of the UCC and the UCCA I had stayed in London after I was discharged from the army in order to work for the CURB and had waived my right to go home at government expense. On the grounds that I had breached our agreement by conducting political activities and setting up the UIS, the UCC refused to pay either my salary or my way home. Although I wrote to the UCC, it kept stalling by saying, "It's not our job. Write to the UCRF." I wrote to the UCRF, and they replied that they hadn't talked to the UCC yet. Months went by, and finally they asked whether they should send the money to me in London. I said, "No, don't send it to me in London because then

I will be subject to British income tax. Deposit the money in my account at the Royal Bank of Canada in Toronto." Later I found out that they had not sent it. Even our treasurer, George Kluchevsky, wrote to Winnipeg to say, "Look, you promised to send Frolick money. What is the matter with you?" They never did send it.

They did not even cover all my expenses. When I went to meetings with the French committee, my expenses were reimbursed, but I paid my own way to Edinburgh, where I delivered the keynote speech at a conference of Ukrainians who had served in the Polish armed forces, and to Dublin. Who wouldn't be angry under the circumstances? I had given a year and a half of my time and had spent all my own money working for the cause and then had been whipped like a dog.

And yet I am proud that I played a part in one of the most fascinating chapters in Ukrainian-Canadian history. The CURB faced enormous problems with only meagre resources. The success it achieved was due to two simple facts: the uniforms of the victorious armed forces worn by those associated with the bureau opened doors to the highest seats of power, and the cause was humanitarian and just.

CHAPTER 10

CANADA AGAIN

In December 1946, using my military connections, I booked passage from Glasgow to Halifax on a "commercial aircraft carrier." These ships had been invented during the war. They carried grain in their holds and had short flight-decks. They would take on grain in Canada, the United States or Argentina, then join armed conveys to cross the Atlantic. To protect themselves against attack, they carried anti-aircraft guns, torpedoes, depth charges and warplanes that could be catapulted from the flight-deck. When the war ended, the carriers were used to haul grain between Canada and Britain. On my trip the hold was filled with water, and the numerous cabins for the plane crews and anti-aircraft gunners were almost empty. I was given the surgeon's cabin. It was one of the better cabins and was located on deck. But the ship, having been built in wartime, was creaky and leaky, and the mid-winter gales tossed it around like a cork. Although my cabin was above deck and the portholes were closed, seawater poured in. I slept in the top bunk, and every morning I would have to wait until the cabin boy had come in and bailed out the water that was sloshing about before I could leave the cabin.

My salary in the service had been considerable, but I had spent all of it while I was working for the CURB, and when I arrived in Canada, I was penniless. To go to Winnipeg I had to borrow money from my mother. I intended to explain to the UNF what had happened during the war, especially the split between the Bandera and Melnyk factions of the OUN, and to try to persuade the UNF to adopt a positive attitude towards the UPA and the UHVR or at least not adopt a Melnykite position of complete hostility. I also wanted to meet with the UCC to demand an explanation for its actions and to claim the remuneration to which I was entitled. I therefore collected all the documents I could muster so that the UCC could not weasel out of its commitment.

When I landed in Halifax, I took a train to Montreal, where I visited the local UNF people in order to give them a report about the situation in Europe. But when I went to the UNF hall, a member of the local executive told me confidentially that he could not let me speak because the national executive had ordered all the branches not to give me a forum.

I had worked more closely with the Toronto people as a member of the eastern executive and had corresponded with some of them while I was in London. They were very civil and were genuinely interested in my views. They told me that they had received information about the split, but it may have been one-sided and prejudiced. If my version was correct, they were prepared to reassess their position, and they insisted that I go to Winnipeg and present my case to the national executive of the UNF.

The reception in Winnipeg was entirely different. The local members of the national executive – Macenko, Gulay, Kossar, Lev Wowk and Eustace Wasylyshen – assembled at the UNYF office. They glared at me from the moment I walked in, and I had barely begun my speech when Gulay, the president of the Ukrainian War Veterans' Association, interrupted me with a vituperative tirade. How could we ally ourselves with people who had killed their brothers, he asked. The others would not listen when I tried to explain. Outshouting one another, they roared that they were not interested in what I had to say. I was a traitor, they yelled. Perhaps I was a traitor to the UNF, I replied, but my allegiance was to my people, not to an organization.

I had a calmer, although equally unfruitful, meeting with Kushnir. He invited me to his house, generously poured drinks and made all sorts of promises, but gave me no real satisfaction. When I asked for my salary, he said that I was entitled to it, and the matter would be reviewed. I said that the failure to pay me was a breach of our contract. If I wasn't paid, I would take the matter to court. Of course, I wouldn't do that, Kushnir said to me. How would it look in the eyes of non-Ukrainians if I sued the UCC?

People would forget that I had a legitimate grievance and would blame me. I realized that Kushnir was right and did not sue. I might win in court but would be smeared in the eyes of the community. My attempts to pursue the matter out of court brought no results. Instead of settling the debt, the UCC tried to justify itself by dismissing me after I had resigned and alleging that there were irregularities in the financial records, although I had nothing to do with the bookkeeping and the only irregularities were Panchuk's.

Then the UNF began to smear me. In Winnipeg, I had met friends from the UCSA – John Swystun, who had been a captain in the army service corps, Nick Malanchuk, who was a flying officer, and other people. Swystun and his wife threw a party for me at their house and invited my friends. We ate, drank and played bridge. At the next annual convention of the UNF, Kossar attacked me in a speech. "Frolick claims to be a nationalist," he said, "but when he arrived in Winnipeg, the first person who greeted him and who organized a banquet in his honour was Swystun." Few people knew John Swystun, a young fellow who had gone overseas when he was eighteen or nineteen and had come back four years later, but everyone knew his father, Wasyl Swystun, who had resigned from the vice-presidency of the UNF in May 1943 and then in February 1945 had sided with the Communists. The inference was clear: I, too, was a Communist.

I thought it was abominable that Ukrainians who endorsed the idea of freedom for the Ukrainian people would not support the UPA in its struggle and were even trying to denigrate it in any possible way. That was when I decided to establish a newspaper that would inform people in Canada about events in Ukraine.

I chose the name *Homin Ukrainy,* or "Ukrainian Echo," because I like literature and the word *homin* has a poetic ring to it. In this newspaper, we who were so far away would echo what was happening in Ukraine. And *homin* is not quite an echo. It is softer, more a memory of a voice or a murmur. In distinction to the UCC, which posed as the leader and spokesman of all Ukrainians, we would only support whatever was happening there and convey the message of fighting Ukraine to people here.

The question of an editor was the most important issue to be resolved. I wrote to Munich for advice and was told that Roman Rakhmanny, the editor of the Ukrainian Press Service, would be sent. We scheduled the publication of the first issue in the expectation of Rakhmanny's arrival, but some hitch prevented him from coming. Since Dmytro Dontsov was now living in Montreal, I turned to him. I wrote to him, argued with him and even went to see him in Montreal. Dontsov said that he could write articles from time to time or even be a contributing editor, but refused to be the editor-in-chief. I therefore engaged Michael Sosnowsky to be the editor for the time being. Eventually Rakhmanny arrived, and I had a problem to resolve. Since he had started the paper and was doing a good job, Sosnowsky felt insulted by being asked to step down in favour of Rakhmanny. I had to use much tact and diplomacy to heal the wound. Eventually Sosnowsky and Rakhmanny came to work well together.

Homin Ukrainy began to appear in December 1948. As the publisher, I paid for the printing of the first half a dozen issues out my own pocket. In 1949, when the *Liga Vyzvolennia Ukrainy,* or League for the Liberation of Ukraine (LLU), was formed, it became the publisher. OUN members were required to subscribe to the paper, and as more of them arrived in Canada the financial burden was spread out.

The transfer of the paper was not without friction. I did not view the paper as my private business and financed it only because the job had to be done. No funds came from Munich. On the contrary, funds flowed from Canada to Munich, which gave us budgets that we had to meet. Finances were always a bone of contention between the leaders in Munich and me. They were trying to kill the goose that laid the golden egg and would not give us a chance to establish ourselves.

I had written a programmatic statement for the first issue of *Homin Ukrainy* in which I announced that it would be a spokesman for the UPA, the UHVR and the OUN. Some of the Canadian leaders agreed with me that the paper should continue as a voice for all three bodies and not become a mouthpiece of the LLU. But a faction headed by Roman Malashchuk gave its first allegiance to the OUN and not to the UPA or the UHVR. It was a question of emphasis. Was *Homin Ukrainy* supposed to serve only the needs of the OUN? Or was it also supposed to serve the UPA and the UHVR, which in my view were greater than the OUN? Not believing that the LLU would change the emphasis of the paper, I handed it over, and to his dying day Ivan Eliashevsky, another member of the OUN who had come to Canada, thought that I had betrayed our principles and made my greatest mistake. And it is true that the UPA and the UHVR were lost in the shuffle. The OUN was now being reconstituted in Canada. The structure of the organization was such that every member's superior in Europe knew his whereabouts and would be informed if he was leaving for Canada. The first post-war immigrants came to work in the logging industry, the sugar-beet industry or as domestics. People would sign a one- or two-year contract, pass a physical examination and then report to their superiors in the OUN that they were leaving. They would be given the code name and address of a person to get in touch with. At first, I was the contact person. Later, when we had built up our structure, others were delegated. When we had registered enough members, we decided to form the LLU. We envisaged it as the only organization, but Munich said that we had to retain a parallel underground network. I said that this made no sense. It would be more efficient to have a single organization. The structure of the OUN had been shaped by the circumstances in pre-war Europe, where an anti-government movement could survive only if the members knew as little about one another as possible. What was the point of conspiracy in Canada, where we could freely carry on our work?

I remember that Stepan Rozhko came from Winnipeg to Toronto to establish a bookstore. He found a tiny place on Bathurst Street, just north of Queen Street, and then came to ask me how he could obtain a permit to sell books. I told him that he didn't need a permit. "You don't need a permit, you don't have to go to the police or the authorities?" he asked. No, I said. If he was going to sell cigarettes, milk or food, he would have to go to city hall and pay five dollars for a license. Rozhko went to city hall and bought a vendor's permit. He was an intelligent man, but he had been brought up in Poland, a semi-police state where written permission was required for everything, and could not conceive of a free society in which you can do whatever you want as long as you don't run afoul of the law.

Similarly, having never lived in a country like Canada, Bandera and the other leaders in Munich could not understand the conditions here. They had lived with their organizational structure for so long that it had become a ritual, an inseparable part of their ideology. In Ukraine they had developed a tight chain of command, which was ultimately responsible first to a collegium and then, under Bandera, to one man. I found the constant need to report up the chain of command hard to take. If a person is appointed to do a job, then let him do it. Why send him directives when you don't know the conditions that he's working in? How can you maintain day-to-day control over an organization from Munich? I concluded that any organization here, whether conspiratorial or legal, had to be autonomous. I also found the practice of calling fellow members by code name a childish charade. Why should I have called Rozhko by a party pseudonym when we knew each other's real names and were both listed in the telephone book?

The first president of the LLU was Yakiw Nesterenko, an Eastern Ukrainian who had served as an officer in the Petliura army. He was one of the few survivors of the battle at Bazar in November 1921, when 443 soldiers of the Ukrainian National Republic were taken prisoner by the Red Army and 359 were executed. Nesterenko went to Czechoslovakia, studied chemistry and then came to Canada. He was one of the first scientists to work with radioactive material and eventually died of skin cancer. Since the LLU was to be a mass organization, it needed members who would support the UPA and the UHVR but would not necessarily belong to the OUN. I picked Nesterenko to head the LLU because although he was a patriot, he did not belong to any political group, and I thought that he would give the LLU a non-immigrant and non-OUN flavour. He served only one term – he felt that he was not cut out to be the president of an organization – but we remained friends.

Outside the LLU, there was a good deal of hostility against me, much of it fueled by Kossar. Shortly after Gloria and I were married, we went to a Ukrainian wedding reception at a Polish hall on Queen Street. A newly arrived Melnyk supporter began screaming at me and calling me a murderer and traitor. Gloria was shocked and could not understand the man's passion and hatred. Later the enmity cooled off because a struggle between the Melnyk faction and the old guard broke out in the UNF. Just as the Banderites had taken over the LLU, so the Melnykites were fighting for control of the UNF and were kicking out everyone who did not agree with them. Kossar himself was thrown out, too, and died a forgotten man in 1970.

I finally broke with the OUN in 1952. There had been tension in Europe in 1946, when I first met Father Hryniokh, Mykola Lebed, and Yurii Lopatynsky, who had been a high-ranking officer in the UPA. Even then a few of them had said, in a bleak way that I did not understand then, "Remember, the UHVR is the main thing." To me this seemed obvious, because the UHVR was the government, as it were, and the OUN was a political party, but these people were telling me to put my allegiances in order.

My departure from the OUN had nothing to do with the split in the Bandera faction, and I left on my own initiative. The circumstances were entirely different from those in which I had left the CURB. I left in a civilized way, without recriminations, mud-slinging or back-stabbing. I wrote a letter to Bandera in which I said that I saw no need for a conspiratorial network in Canada. Make the organization open and let anyone who agrees with its principles to join it. Bandera replied that we would not be able to control an open organization. I asked him what difference that made. Uniformity of thought could not be imposed. If people agreed with us, they should be welcomed. If they changed their minds, they should be free to leave. Bandera did not agree. I told him that I knew better than he did what would work best in Canada and would have to leave the organization. And I think I was right. The LLU had great potential and could have given leadership to the whole Ukrainian Canadian community. Instead it withdrew into its own shell, permitted only members of the OUN to be in the executive and made people who were not members feel unwelcome.

The official transfer of power took place in my bedroom. I had a disk problem and was in and out of hospitals, and during one of these bouts with my bad back, the executive board came to see me, and I transferred power to Roman Malashchuk.

In the August 1953 federal election I ran as a Conservative in Trinity, a working-class riding that had voted Conservative only once in its history. Immediately after the war a returning officer with a flying cross had been elected by ninety-one votes. He held the riding one term, and then it went back to voting Liberal. By 1953 I had been graduated from the University of Toronto and was working towards a master's degree in Russian. I would have received my degree in May, except that in February the president of the Conservative association in the Trinity riding asked me if I would run in the coming election. I accepted the offer and left graduate school to campaign.

Michael Starr had been elected in the by-election of 1952, and I was only the second Ukrainian to run as a federal candidate in Ontario. Ukrainians responded in their inimitable fashion. When one man is successful, they try to cut him down to size.

The Orange hall, where the nomination meeting was taking place, was small, and only sixty to eighty people were present. Suddenly a group including Pohorecky, the brother of the editor of the *Novyi shliakh,* and Stephen Pawluk, who was the president of the Ukrainian Legion and a former UNF member, stormed into the hall. They were not members of the riding association and had not bothered to find out how the political process works in Canada.

"Wait a minute," the chairman said. "This is a nominating convention of the Trinity PC riding association. Who are you?"

"We have a candidate," they replied. "Steve Pawluk."

Robert Martin, who was the president of the riding associa tion, made fun of the name. "Paluka?" he said. "Have you got a Paluka? Who's he?"

I stood there cringing while these fellows were arguing with the president that they had a right to come to the meeting because they had a candidate.

Nesterenko, who was my biggest backer in the campaign, approached the group. "Why come here?" he said. "If you want to nominate Pawluk, go to Spadina or some other riding, but don't cause trouble here."

Pawluk's supporters persisted. When it was finally made clear to them that they could not nominate Pawluk, they demanded the right to ask questions.

"What sort of questions do you want to ask, questions about the Conservative party's policies?" Martin said.

"No," said Pohorecky. "We have certain questions to ask of the candidate you want to nominate, Mr. Frolick. We want to find out how he was able to leave the Soviet Union and come here when everybody knows that no one leaves the Soviet Union unless he is sent here."

What a vicious innuendo! I was accused of being an agent in the presence of people who were about to nominate me and who knew nothing about the Soviet Union or communism or the UNF.

The riding association executives then said that they would call the police and have the group ejected. This was not a public meeting, but a gathering of Tory party members. Shouting, hooting and threatening, the group left the building.

That was not the end of it. Once the campaign began, I tried to get the support of the Eastern European communities. In a political sense, that support meant little, but I still thought more in hybrid Ukrainian-Canadian terms than in purely Canadian terms and felt an obligation to ask all the newspapers and organizations for their endorsement. I remember that I was invited to address the Polish nationalists grouped around *Glos Polski* and *Związek Narodowy*. I decided that I had to go because there were many Poles in the riding at that time. I would win them over by speaking Polish. With the possible exception of the Communist party, they had never had a non-Polish candidate address them in Polish. When I had finished my speech, I asked whether there were any questions. "What is your opinion on the *kresy wschodnie*?" one Pole asked provocatively. *Kresy wschodnie*, or "eastern borderland," was a Polish term for Western Ukraine.

I gave the only possible answer. We all faced a *fait accompli*, I said. That part of the former Polish republic was now incorporated into the Ukrainian SSR, and we in the Trinity riding were not going to determine the status of the region.

There was worse to come. When I told the UNF that I was campaigning, I was invited to address a meeting of the executive. Stefaniia Sawchuk, a big wheel in the UNF and the World Congress of Ukrainian Women's Organizations, was there. Her question to me was typical of a certain mentality in the community. "If you're elected and you're asked by the government whom to recognize as the representative of Ukraine, the Ukrainian National Council or the UHVR, what will your recommendation be?"

I told her that the question would never arise. Nobody would ask me or her or even Canada to choose the future government of Ukraine. The Ukrainians themselves would decide that.

Sawchuk was determined to get an answer. "But if we were asked," she said. "How would you reply?"

In the election I ran against L. Conacher from the Liberal Party, H. Voaden from the CCF and Tim Buck from the Labour Progressive Party. Conacher, who was a famous athlete, won the election. I came in second, and Voaden was fourth. Buck, who was the leader of the Communist Party of Canada, managed to get about two thousand votes, a respectable showing, though much weaker than the Communists' showing in the 1945 and 1949 elections.

While I was campaigning in the riding, I passed the Ukrainian Catholic church on Bathurst Street and saw that Conacher's campaign poster had been put up on the notice board. I felt terrible. Conacher had no intelligence and made no contribution to the country or to the Ukrainian community. His absenteeism in the House of Commons was notorious, and he opened his mouth only when he was honoured as athlete of the half century and stood up to acknowledge the congratulations. And yet my own people were supporting him.

Father Michael Horoshko, a Ukrainian Catholic priest whom I had met at the UCSA, came around. I pointed to the poster and said, "Look what your people are doing."

"Damn it," Horoshko said. "I'll go fix it."

The assistant priest in the parish was a recent immigrant who had been my fellow student at the *gymnasium* in Stanyslaviv. "How could I have said no?" he told Horoshko. "Conacher came over and gave me a set of golf clubs." A set of golf clubs was the price of a Ukrainian priest. When you add all these things up, you wonder who you're working for and whether the effort is justified. Thank God not every one is like that and there are fine people in the community.

Electoral politics reinforced my conviction that Ukrainian Canadians could achieve power only by united effort. Paul Yuzyk had a similar idea when he fostered the idea of a non-English and non-French "third force" in Canada, but my concept came first. Even though I was only twenty-two years old at the time of the UCC congress in 1943, I had tried to promote the notion of a superstructure, an umbrella of umbrellas. We had the UCC, and the Polish Congress and the Canadian Jewish Congress had come into existence. The Poles had sent greetings to the UCC congress and had proposed co-operation. The UCC rejected the offer, not because of the historic antagonisms between Ukrainians and Poles or because there might be arguments over Western Ukraine, but for the shortsighted reason that Ukrainians in Canada had nothing to gain from such an alliance. Later the Baltic Federation approached the UCC with a similar proposal to work together to achieve common goals, and again the UCC spurned the request on the grounds that the Balts wanted to ride on its coat-tails. The UCC was very important, I was told. It had influence in Ottawa, and the Balts would only use it to make political capital. As the Ukrainian proverb has it, "The satiated one does not want to know the hungry one."

Relations between French Canadians and Ukrainians have been marked by a similar failure to appreciate the other's point of view. Both groups feel deprived of the rights that they consider their due, yet they have been unable to find common ground, and each side is hostile to the aspirations of the other. One Western MP of Ukrainian origin had high hopes of reaching a modus *vivendi* with French-speaking politicians, only to see his hopes dashed to smithereens. And my friend, the late Anthony Hlynka, was almost obsessed with his self-imposed mission to seek an alliance with politicians from Quebec in the struggle against the WASP establishment for the aspirations of the French and the Ukrainians. I remember the keen disappointment that he felt when he realized that French Canadians were less disposed than the English-speaking majority to grant any further rights or to redress any inequalities. Convinced of the righteousness of their cause and certain that they had political power in Quebec, the French proved to be too arrogant to turn for help to anyone else.

In 1953, after my venture into politics, I resurrected my idea of Eastern European solidarity and set about forming the Mutual Cooperation League (MCL). With some difficulty, I persuaded the UCC to recognize me as its representative – though only of the Toronto branch, and not of the national headquarters in Winnipeg – and got in touch with the Lithuanians, Estonians and Latvians. They agreed in principle to my proposal. Then I approached the Poles and had a hell of a time selling the idea to them, but in the end succeeded. The Canadian Hungarian Association delegated George Kollontai, who had served with the Hungarian army on the Eastern front during the Second World War. When the Hungarians were withdrawing from Ukraine in 1944, Kollontai negotiated a truce between the Hungarian high command and the UPA and and left behind weapons for the Ukrainians. The Czechs and Slovaks were a problem because of the animosity between them. Two Slovak representatives joined us: Milan Jakubec, who served as secretary when we were constituted as an organization, and Dr. Joseph Kirschbaum, who later became a big wheel in Denison Mines. Kirschbaum had served as a diplomat in the Tiso government under the Nazis in Slovakia. He had a lot of flack from the Czechoslovak government. Since the Slovaks had joined, the Czechs were disturbed, and when we finally got a Czech representative to join us, he was never active. There was a similar problem with the Yugoslavs. We had Slovenian and Macedonian representatives, but when the Croatians joined, the Serbs would not come in.

I also invited the Canadian Jewish Congress to join the MCL.

Ukrainian-Jewish relations have long been marred by prejudice, ignorance and ill-will on both sides. For Jews, the obstacle to better relations is the alleged anti-Semitism of Bohdan Khmelnytsky, the seventeenth-century Ukrainian leader, and Symon Petliura, the twentieth-century politician, and the countenancing of these positions by most present-day Ukrainians.

On the Ukrainian side, the stumbling block has been the allegation that the Jews have always sided with the oppressors of the Ukrainian people and that they are indifferent, or even hostile, to the Ukrainian struggle for self-determination. Perhaps it was these prejudices that prompted the Canadian Jewish Congress to refuse to join on the grounds that its objectives were different from those of the Lithuanian, Ukrainian and Polish federations.

The MCL was a sad disappointment. The idea was premature, and none of the organizations were prepared to back it to the utmost. Small as our needs were, we did need funds for paper and postage. Although I had obtained the approval of the local UCC to represent it in the MCL, I was unable to get it to contribute to the budget and was forced to resign. The MCL carried on for a while without me and then fell apart.

We Ukrainians, I have come to realise, feel so strongly about retaining our language and culture because we feel threatened by assimilation and extinction. We cannot look to a sovereign state, as the Jews and the Western and Southern Europeans can, and we see that in our homeland the Ukrainian spirit is being systematically and deliberately destroyed. We are a branch that has been lopped off the trunk and must find a way not to wither away and die. Our mission on this continent is to preserve the cultural values of the entire Ukrainian nation.

Understandable and laudable though this determination may be, it has also produced a deep-seated anxiety. We feel threatened on all sides. The fear is reflected in our attitudes, our self-image and our organizations. Criticism – even constructive criticism – is discouraged. To criticize is to destroy. If you criticize, you risk being branded as a traitor because you are playing into the hands of our enemies. As if they were unaware of our weaknesses and fail to exploit them! Because of our siege mentality, we conceal our shortcomings even from ourselves. In emphasizing only the positive, we are not beyond twisting facts to suit the image we want to project. Consequently, many myths and fantasies have accumulated. In the long run, they achieve a result opposite to the one sought.

It has become an annual ritual, for example, to commemorate the rebirth of an independent Ukrainian state in 1918. But why did it not endure? Speaker after speaker will explain the collapse by enumerating the overwhelming enemy forces arrayed against the young state, blaming the Entente for failing to come to its aid or arguing that its troops were vanquished by a typhus epidemic. But did typhus spare the armies of such smaller countries as the Baltic states? Did it benevolently leave alone the armies of the Red and White Russians? Was Lithuania, a country of only several millions, not opposed in its liberation struggle by Polish and Russian foes of every hue? The answer is that we failed because we did not want freedom badly enough to fight, to suffer and even to die if need be. Too many refused to support their government and to risk life and limb.

Because of our tendency to fictionalize and to sweep unpleasant aspects of our past under the rug, we portray the settlement of the Canadian West by our pioneering forefathers, their struggle with a hostile human and physical environment, as a story of joy, hope and optimism. This simplistic and romantic version bears little relation to historical truth.

We Ukrainians also have the unfortunate habit of starting history from the creation of our favourite organization. Although it may be true, as the Ukrainian proverb has it, that "every gypsy praises his own children," it is ludicrous to assert that nothing of consequence was accomplished before the UNF, say, came into being or before the last wave of DPs landed on these shores.

Because of our gut-felt anti-communism we refuse to concede that the pro-Communist organizations may have made a contribution of worth, if only with their orchestras, choirs and Ukrainian-language schools. The involvement of Ukrainians in the Winnipeg general strike is unmentionable because we are loath to present ourselves as radicals. Even the role of the socialists in our early history in Canada is buried deep from sight. Yet it is a fact that the first Ukrainian-Canadian leaders were socialists and that they laid the foundations of our present-day organizations. Similarly, our religious bias prevents us from acknowledging the part played by the Ukrainian Protestant churches.

In the common view, modern Ukrainian-Canadian history begins with the emergence of the Ukrainian Orthodox church and such organizations as the USRL, the UNF, the Hetmanites and the BUC. This was a turbulent period, marked by religious controversy and ideological batles. The clash between the Catholics and the Orthodox was so emotionally charged and dragged on for so long that this page of our history cannot be hidden. Yet the tendency in recent decades has been to play down the strife, to pretend that it never happened. Why? Does a mature adult have to be ashamed of his acts as an adolescent and to create psychological problems by denying childhood sins?

Then there was the violence between the Communists and the nationalists, particularly when the Second World War broke out and the government outlawed Communist organizations and sold their halls, mainly to the UNF. This was an intense ideological struggle between two opposing philosophies. But how can one explain the violent fights and the raids on each other's halls between the UNF and the Hetmanites? How many people today know about the suit that went all the way to the Supreme Court of Canada involving two organizations that professed essentially similar political goals? And how many people know about the extensive litigation between the *Narodny Dim* halls and the Orthodox church or the USRL arising out of conflicting claims to ownership of those halls?

We are taught that this fratricidal warring came to an end when the UCC was created in the early 1940s. The UCC, we are told, came into being as an answer to the longing for unity on the part of all Ukrainians. People suddenly realized the folly of internal strife and perceived the advantages of concerted action. Therefore, the story goes, the leaders of the community gave birth to this highest and most perfect organizational form in which all groups, the Communists excepted, joined to produce a united front. But what are the facts?

It was the federal government that stepped in to bring the

warring factions together. To justify this intervention, another myth was created: that unity was necessary for the survival of democracy and the prosecution of the war effort. But when the existing organizations coalesced into two representative bodies, both of which claimed to speak for the majority of Ukrainian Canadians, Ottawa and London sent in Simpson, Kirkconnell and Philipps to bring everyone together. In the interests of unity? In the interests of the war effort? But why was Philipps of the British secret service sent in? Why was the British government concerned? The reason was that both the Canadian and British governments feared that Germany might launch a pro-Ukrainian policy and create an independent Ukrainian state. How would Ottawa and London deal with almost half a million Ukrainians whom they could not control? The Ukrainians were too numerous and too scattered to be interned, as the Japanese were.

Although the UCC was created in such circumstances, I cannot be overly critical of it. I do fault it, however, on several grounds. The UCC has become ossified in its undemocratic mold, and reform and modernization to make it more responsive to changing needs seem impossible. Profound changes have occurred since the UCC was created, and yet tired old men have hung on to the reins of leadership long after their energy and enthusiasm were exhausted. One of the greatest sins that I ascribe to the UCC leaders is that by retaining power for two generations they have denied a role in the mainstream of Ukrainian affairs to the dedicated and idealistic generation that served in the Canadian armed forces in the last war and proved itself to be composed of doers and achievers.

One thread that ran through all my interests was the cause of a free and independent Ukraine. That issue has now faded into the background. During the war years, the idea of dismembering the Soviet Union while it was locked in a life-and-death struggle with nazism gained some prominence. After the war the international situation was more favourable to such an idea. Britain and France ceased to be colonial powers. New states emerged in Asia and Africa. The only remaining colonial power was the Soviet Union. One would have thought that in this climate the question of political independence for Ukraine would have been in the forefront. It was not. The reason was that John Diefenbaker was the only political leader who was interested in the question. Although he raised the matter, even in the United Nations, he was in power for too short a period to give it any impetus. His predecessors and successors had no feeling for the matter. Pierre Trudeau, in particular, made it absolutely clear that he equated Ukraine with Quebec and wanted to hear nothing about the liberation of either. His years in power were catastrophic for the Ukrainian-Canadian community because he was so preoccupied with the French Canadian issue that he excluded all others. But we ourselves were also at fault and lacked strong leadership. At one time, when the Ukrainian-Canadian community was much smaller than it is now, its voice was heard more clearly in Ottawa. Even though the issue of Ukrainian independence may not have fallen on sympathetic ears, other problems did receive attention.

Ukrainian Canadians have suffered from an inferiority complex and a need to prove their loyalty to Canada. They have tried to assert and reassert their attachment to British institutions and symbols, including the crown. But we must not forget that with one or two exceptions the leaders of the UCC were immigrants. The first Ukrainian immigrants had come to Canada with the idea that they would stay only long enough to earn money and then go back to Ukraine, buy land and enjoy a better life. Later immigrants came with the intention of staying in Canada permanently and faced the difficulties of integrating into Canadian society. I believe that had other people been in the leadership of the UCC such difficulties would have been avoided. The need to assert loyalty was produced by the fear of being interned, as had happened during the First World War. No native-born Canadians had been interned then, and the naturalized Canadians in the Ukrainian-Canadian leadership produced a distorted image of the community because they expressed the fears and feelings of only one group, the immigrants. And even then the immigrant group did not constitute the majority of the Ukrainian-Canadian population.

All these factors combined, I believe, to produce the situation in which we find ourselves. We also erred tactically. Trudeau made it clear that he would give a sympathetic hearing only to questions of human rights. The Ukrainian community shifted its emphasis from rights for the nation, which Trudeau would not hear about, to rights for individuals. So only "humanitarian" matters were raised in the last fifteen years. We have focussed on them for so long that we have forgotten national rights, and even if the climate changes, we will still continue to address only questions of dissent in the Soviet Union, of helping the dissidents and criticizing the Soviet Union for not adhering to the 1976 Helsinki accords, forgetting that they also contained commitments to self-determination and other matters that are far more important than the preservation of personal civil liberties. Yet even this aspect is not pursued with as much conviction and zeal as it deserves.

My career in public affairs ranged from party politics – I ran in three elections, two federal and one provincial – to my involvement in *Homin Ukrainy,* the League for the Liberation of Ukraine, the Mutual Co-operation League, the Ukrainian Professional and Businessmen's Association and the Chair of Ukrainian Studies at the University of Toronto. Most people follow one particular interest. I am happy that I succeeded in most of my endeavours.

I find no difficulty in reconciling my Canadianism with my commitment to freedom for a people that deserves it. Surely a case can be made that Ukraine, which has existed for a thousand years and has all the historical, cultural and linguistic dimensions that are usually associated with nationhood, deserves to be de-colonized. Why should one nation rule over another, and why should the Ukrainians or Georgians (who have a long and glorious history) be subjugated by the Russians? I have no problem in supporting what I perceive to be morally and historically right. It is a duty to help less fortunate individuals, groups or nations. So too with my Canadianism. I do not think of myself as a lesser Canadian and do not suffer from any inferiority complex in this respect. Perhaps I have even contributed more to Canadian society than the average Canadian through my involvement for over thirty years in Canadian political affairs.